D. White

W9-CCP-260

The Outrageous Outdoor Games Book

Bob Gregson

133 Group Projects, Games, and Activities

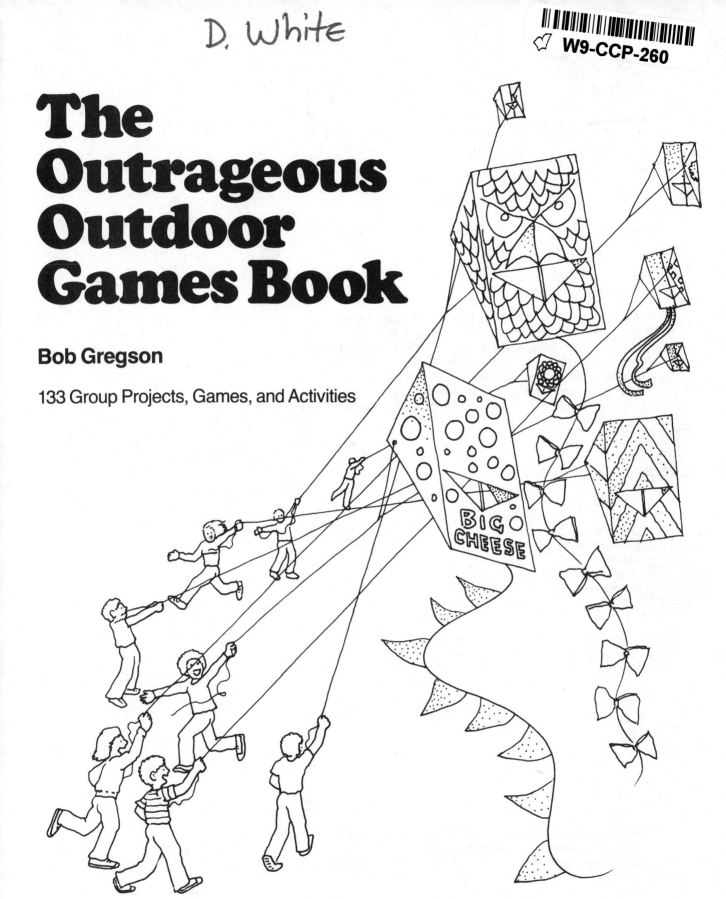

A Learning Ideabook™

Fearon Teacher Aids
a division of
David S. Lake Publishers
Belmont, California

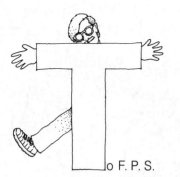

o F. P. S.

Acknowledgments

A special thank you to *Bernie DeKoven*; *Peter Swanson*;
Tom Zink; *Frank Self*; *the Teacher Center of New Haven*; *my
family—Judy Fechino*, *Chris Gregson*, *Mark Gregson*; *and
many playful friends—Faith, Cindy, Dorothy, Tracey, Ann,
Bill, Paul, Susan, Joan, Donald, Judith, Jim, Arabel, Jakob,
Harrison, Robin, Glenn, Yvonne, Michael, Larry, Chuck,
Linda, Sidney, Irwin, Debbie, Suzy, Margaret, and Mara*.

Editorial director: Ina Tabibian
Editor: Gustavo Medina
Designer: Susan True
Cover designer: Susan True
Illustrator: Bob Gregson
Design director: Eleanor Mennick
Production editor: Anne Lewis

Copyright © 1984 by David S. Lake Publishers, 19 Davis Drive,
Belmont, California 94002. All rights reserved. No part of this book
may be reproduced by any means, transmitted, or translated into a
machine language without written permission from the publisher.

ISBN–0–8224–5099–2
Library of Congress Catalog Card Number: 83-62564
Printed in the United States of America.
1.9 8 7

CONTENTS

INTRODUCTION

Play is a response to our individual needs for expression. It helps us understand who and what we are by allowing us to explore and enhance our physical abilities, feelings, intuitions, skills, and intellectual capabilities. Through play we develop an awareness of our personal identity and appreciate our connection with others. Intuitively we know that play is important. Yet, we may not be able to describe it or its function. Play is a way to expand our lives by testing our desires and fantasies in a safe environment.

We play all the time. Even as we work we are playing—giving ourselves small challenges, structuring games and rewards, daydreaming, thinking up ideas and fantasies—in order to change work into fun and to make it more tolerable.

We play to work better. The opposite is also true. As the challenges of play become greater, we find ourselves working harder to develop specific skills and ideas that fulfill us. Play is the motivator. Work is what we do to maintain ourselves physically. Play is the attitude and the action we need for spiritual survival.

The *Outrageous Outdoor Games Book* is for play leaders who are organizing groups of 10 to 30 players, 6 to 16 years old. It's a collection of games and projects that maximize opportunities for outdoor play, yet minimize preparation and planning. Activities are designed to invite group interaction as well as develop individual self-expression. Some activities are traditional games with new twists. Many others are brand new. All are easy to do and are adaptable to a variety of situations and skill levels.

Outdoor play can happen anywhere—yards, fields, sidewalks, beaches, parks, parking lots, and playgrounds. For active players who like to run, yell, and jump, outdoor spaces are invitations to somersaults in the grass and hopping races on the sidewalk.

Outdoor play opens up new creative vistas for the imagination. For young players, an empty yard or a parking lot can be a laboratory in which to try out ideas and to shape their own worlds. For older players, it can be a way to see the world from a different and fresher perspective. For adults who have not fully allowed themselves to play in years, the novelty of forgotten physical sensations, the excitement of adventure, and the surprise at how much fun it is to let go are tonics that renew the spirit and reawaken the body.

Play is fun when it challenges us mentally, physically, and emotionally by presenting something which we have never done before and which will reward us with a positive outcome. Play is successful when it provides a variety of choices which engage us in a number of ways so that we can't predict the exact outcome. When a game is predictable, there is nothing else to learn and it becomes boring. When this happens, a different game is needed that will appeal to our needs for novelty, knowledge, and nurture.

Often, play or the reasons for play are invisible. For example, a player building a tower out of cardboard boxes may be:

- Seeing how high he or she can reach
- Seeing how tall the tower can be built before it collapses
- Arranging the boxes to suit an aesthetic need
- Trying to balance the boxes to create a new and different structure
- Trying to build a structure large enough in which to sit and hide

A player needs to be able to have some control over the play situation so that he or she can feel safe in playing. At the same time, a player must not have too much control or else the unexpected surprises that make play fun are not likely to occur.

THE PLAY LEADER

The play leader has the multiple responsibilities of being organizer, supervisor, and player. All this is done so the group can feel free to play as spontaneously as possible. The play leader is not a policeperson enforcing laws but a member of the play group with a slightly different role. The leader's participation is a model for others. It's the leader's job to initiate activities, to supply materials, and to create a congenial atmosphere where players can feel secure in expressing themselves.

Every leader has his or her own special style. There are, however, ways that leaders can persuade people to do things they normally wouldn't try. When players trust the leader, they feel comfortable enough to try just about anything. Here are a few qualities that are helpful when leading activities:

Humor

Humor changes the way we see things by exposing us to the ironies of life. It questions the things we hold as sacred and helps make everyone less self-conscious. Don't be afraid to joke with players and even laugh at yourself. Players are gratified when the leader shows obvious enjoyment. Humor changes the focus from intimidation and "having to win" to sharing the fun with others.

Invitation

Willingness to play is central to every game, and players should have the choice to play or not to play. Invitations are a sign that you would like to share an experience with everyone. Demands are forceful attempts to control the group and to limit each player's freedom of choice. If players don't seem to respond to your invitation, suggest a few games and invite them to choose one.

Sensitivity

Be aware of mood changes within the group. If players have been playing a long time, they might be ready for a quiet game or a break. If some players seem to be getting restless, it might be good to try a more active game. When you are sensitive to the needs of the group, each individual, and your own, a comfortable direction will evolve naturally.

Flexibility

Being flexible means you have to be able to adapt immediately to situations in order to keep the group energy moving in a productive direction. But don't worry if something fails. Instead, involve players so that they themselves become responsible for their own fun and move on to other choices.

As the play session continues, the role of the play leader shifts to one of encouragement, reinforcement, and maintenance. As players become more involved in a game or activity, the play leader can keep an overview—readjusting boundaries and rules as necessary in order to help players play as well as they can.

Safety Awareness

At times children become so enthusiastic about a game that they accidentally hurt themselves. When children don't know their limits and overextend themselves, the play leader must help define or redefine those limits. Everyone should feel physically and psychologically secure. Begin the period carefully with activities that are not risky and have an easy pace. As players become more and more confident, raise the level of risk so that it corresponds to their abilities. But never hesitate to stop a game if you feel that excitement is leading to injury. Remind everyone to be careful of others so nobody gets hurt.

As children attend to their own safety, they can also begin to focus on how their playing affects others. The safety of players is the most important responsibility of the play leader. If an activity seems dangerous or out of control, children won't want to play.

Safety also depends on the type of activity being played. The elements of an activity may need to be adapted to fit within the limits of a particular space. When this is not possible, an entirely different activity may have to be introduced.

If only one or two children are playing carelessly, it is best to approach them individually so as to not embarrass them. Giving them a greater level of responsibility will redirect their efforts in a positive way.

Even a group of children of the same age will have different levels of ability and interest. Play leaders must carefully adapt activities to fit the level of ability that best suits each group.

PLAY DAYS

Play Days are a direct route to fun. They are well-planned sessions that can change everyday playgrounds into an instant festival. Play Days make ordinary games special by connecting related activities together to create a celebration.

Any day can be a Play Day. It can be as big as a three-ring circus or as short as a ten-minute recess. Here are some simple steps that will change a group of games into a celebration.

REASONS TO CELEBRATE

Before organizing a Play Day, players should decide on something to celebrate. The reason doesn't have to be fancy. You can celebrate *anything*—the first day of school, the arrival of spring, a birthday, an anniversary, an ethnic holiday, or the first grassy field of summer. A theme helps players investigate and direct ideas. Sometimes limitations can be turned into assets. For example, if the play space is small, players can create the "World's Smallest Play Day" with scaled-down activities. Many of the activities in this book have already been grouped into related themes, but feel free to regroup activities in your own special combinations.

WAYS TO CELEBRATE

Once a theme has been decided upon, games and activities are needed to explore and expand it. Have everyone list games and projects associated with the theme. Allow players to be whimsical.

It's not always easy to come up with appropriate games and exciting play ideas. Mistakes are bound to happen. They are part of the process. But the excitement of success will overshadow the failures if players are willing to take the risk.

When the fear of failure tightens up those imagination muscles, then play "Mistake Practice." In "Mistake Practice," being wrong is always right. To begin, gather players into a circle, sit on the grass, and take turns inventing the most entertaining mistakes or ideas doomed to failure. Suggest that players start by looking at everyday things in an unconventional way. For example:

- Driving a car with square wheels
- Trying to fly a six-ton rock by using helium-filled balloons
- Drinking soup with a fork
- Moving the Empire State Building to Indiana
- Filling the Atlantic Ocean with bubble bath
- Lifting the entire group in the air with one hand

It takes creativity to come up with silly answers but no matter what, every player's "mistake" should be met with enthusiasm.

After Mistake Practice, players are usually in the mood to imaginatively solve the more practical problem of what to play on Play Day. When possibilities have been exhausted, begin to group games and activities into categories—Active Games, Quiet Games, and so forth. Weed out the games that aren't directly related to the central theme. Star games that seem to be the most popular.

HOW TO CELEBRATE

After collecting a group of games and activities, plans should be made to present them in an organized manner. Some practical decisions must be made on space, time, and materials. Usually it is best to present large group games in a central location with smaller activities around the border. This way players can come together in the large common space for big group games or still feel connected to everyone while playing in smaller groups on the sidelines.

For special Play Days, big, oversized signs made of cardboard and poster paint make great graphics to define games areas and make the excitement visible. Time is also a consideration. Usually Play Days can last two or three hours before players feel worn out. Creative arts activities can continue throughout the Play Day, while group games will probably change every 15 minutes. Make a list of all the activities to make sure there will be enough to fill the entire play session.

It is best to start off slowly and add activities as the Play Day builds. To end the session, focus on a single group activity that will bring everyone together in one final, exciting burst of unity. The last activity should, in some way, symbolize the feeling that gave everyone so much enjoyment. This is the perfect time to launch the helium balloon sculpture everyone has created or to play the longest cooperative tin can stilt walk ever.

WHO CELEBRATES?

Although these outrageous outdoor games have been adapted to fit most easily into a school program, the following list includes many different groups and programs that have benefitted from the games and celebrations:

Families
Park recreation programs
Recreation centers
Arts and crafts programs
YMCAs and YWCAs
Big Brothers and Little Sisters programs
The Salvation Army
Prisons
Homes for the aged
Hospitals—general and psychiatric
Head Start programs
Libraries
Churches
City-wide arts festivals
Theater programs and groups
Neighborhood and community groups
Camps
Ethnic festivals
Parent-teacher associations
Drug rehabilitation programs
State-run homes for children
Centers for the physically impaired
Corporations and businesses
Day-care centers
Architects and city planners
Museums
Colleges and universities

SUN DAYS

Players will find their place in the sun with these bright games. Activities use the sun's movement, rays, and shadows to transform a sun day into fun play.

SHADOW TRACKS

Players become private eyes as they follow the mysterious movements of the "Shadow." The Shadow has been accused of slowly traveling up and down the sides of the buildings and creeping across playgrounds and yards. Collecting substantial evidence requires an all-day stakeout and should be planned as a supplement to other investigations.

EQUIPMENT

A box of chalk
A clock

SITUATION

A shadow on a paved area

TIME

Intermittently all day

DIRECTIONS

1. For this project you will need the sun, a shadow to trace—such as that of a tree, flagpole, or building—and a paved surface on which to draw with chalk. Give each player a piece of chalk.

2. Start the investigation first thing in the morning. At first, shadows will be stretched out and long. Have players trace whatever shadow is cast on the pavement. In the case of a tree, only the trunk might be cast in the morning, but as the day goes by the shadow will shorten and the leaves and branches will soon appear.

3. Allegedly, shadows get shorter because the sun gets higher in the sky. Private eyes will have to check this out every hour by tracing the shadow and checking the sun's position. As detectives keep tabs on the sun's route, they might notice the shadows shrinking to almost nothing by midday and then reversing their position to grow again.

4. At the end of the day, enough evidence will have been collected to prove without a shadow of a doubt that the Shadow moves.

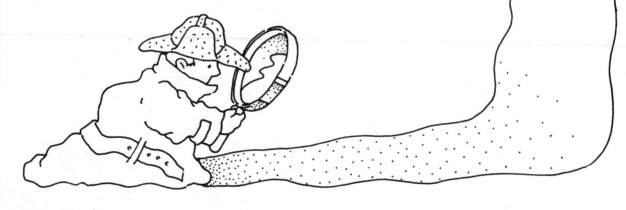

SHADOW TAG

Another sun-sational game is Shadow Tag. Here the sun moves shadows around as players run to and from the direction of the sun.

EQUIPMENT

None

SITUATION

A sunny day on an open playground

TIME

10 minutes

DIRECTIONS

1. One player is chosen to be It. The object of the game is for the person who is It to try and tag another player by stepping on his or her shadow. Define boundaries. No fair running into the shade!

2. When the person who is It steps on someone's shadow, he or she shouts "Sun Tag!"

3. The player whose shadow was tagged becomes the next person to be It, but that player must stand still for three counts before chasing shadows.

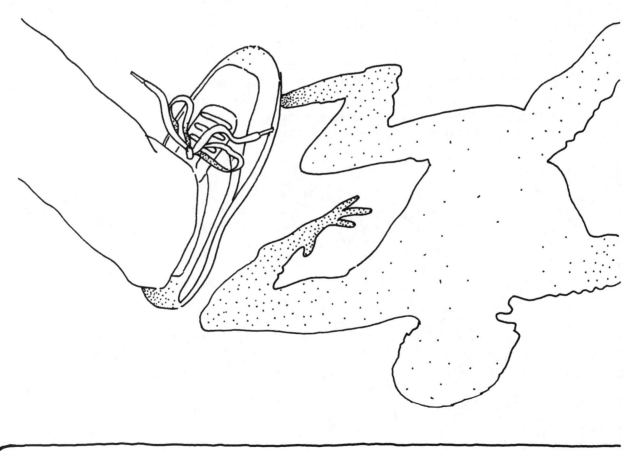

SUN SHADES

You'd think that the idea for Sun Shades would have originated in the sunny South rather than the frozen North. The Eskimos, needing to protect their eyes from the glare reflecting off the snow, invented them. These shades aren't really authentic, but they do use the same Eskimo principles.

EQUIPMENT

An assortment of old shoe boxes, egg boxes,
    corrugated cardboard, construction paper,
    and any heavy paper

Scissors to share
String or twine
Masking tape
Pencils
Rulers to share
An assortment of colored felt markers

SITUATION

Flat surface on which to work

TIME

35 minutes

DIRECTIONS

The basic idea is to create cardboard sun shades. Thin slits or a grid of tiny holes are then cut into them so that a player can look through while glaring reflections are screened out. The style is up to each player. The materials used will affect the design also. For example:

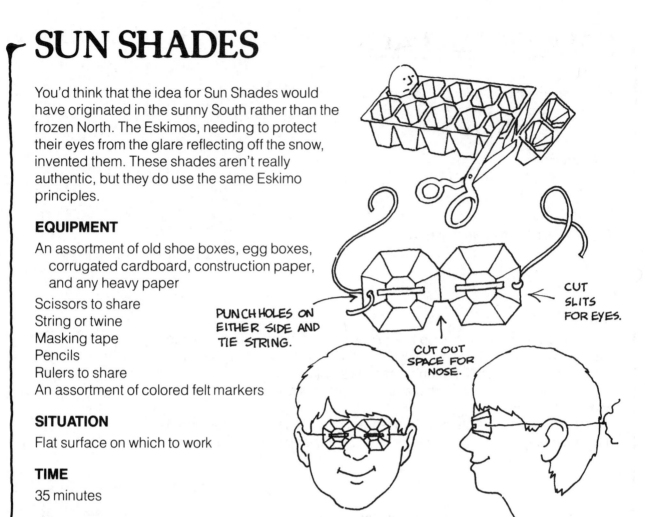

PUNCH HOLES ON EITHER SIDE AND TIE STRING.

CUT SLITS FOR EYES.

CUT OUT SPACE FOR NOSE.

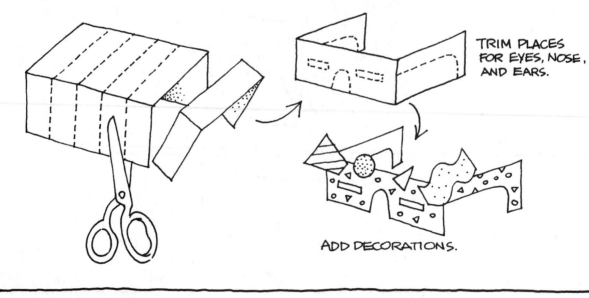

TRIM PLACES FOR EYES, NOSE, AND EARS.

ADD DECORATIONS.

Egg Box Sun Shades

1. Cut a pair of egg holders from an egg carton (one egg carton can make six sun shades).

2. Fit them over the eyes. Cut a place for them to rest on the nose.

3. Cut a 1½- by ⅛-inch slit across each holder for viewing. (Be sure to do this while the shades are on the table, *not* on the player.)

4. To hold shades on, punch holes on either side and tie about 10 inches of string from each hole.

5. Place sun shades on the face and tie the strings together in back of the head.

Shoe Box Sun Shades

1. Cut out the ends of the box. Cut the box into 2-inch strips. (About six pairs of sun shades can be cut from a single shoe box.) Use the folded sides as the earpieces of the shades.

2. Cut a place for the nose, and trim the sides to rest on ears.

3. Cut slits or punch a grid of small holes to see through. Cardboard from shirts, paper plates, or any heavy paper material can be cut and folded to make sun shades. Have players experiment.

4. Decorate sun shades with colorful felt markers or poster paints so that they are as nice to look at as through. For a spectacular spectacle, cover shades with aluminum foil or cover eyepieces with colored cellophane.

THE GLAMOROUS CAT'S EYE DESIGN

THE CIRCUS VERSION

THE SPORTS MODEL

FAN-TASTICS

Being comfortable is a number one priority on hot days. Before the invention of electric fans and air conditioners, people used to wave leaves and feathers to keep the air moving. This increases the evaporation of perspiration and keeps the skin cool. This portable fan is what's needed after an overheated day at play.

CONSTRUCTION PAPER

CARDBOARD

9" 12" 1½" 10"

1. DECORATE.

EQUIPMENT

9" x 12" sheet of construction paper for each player
Masking tape
1½" x 10" cardboard strip for each player
Felt markers in various colors (optional)

SITUATION

Flat surface on a hot day

2. FOLD PAPER INTO ACCORDION PLEATS.

TIME

20 minutes

DIRECTIONS

1. Give each player a 9- by 12-inch sheet of construction paper and a 1½- by 10-inch strip of cardboard. If they'd like, players may decorate either side of their paper with felt marker designs.
2. Fold the paper into an accordion and hold the paper lengthwise.
3. Fold the accordion in half and tape the center together to create a fan.
4. Fold the strip of cardboard in half. Attach the cardboard around the bottom of the fan and wrap it securely with masking tape.
5. Players can use their fans individually or in a group. Make a human wind machine by gathering everyone into a circle and giving each player a turn to stand in the center while everyone fans away.

3. FOLD AND TAPE CENTER.

4. FOLD CARDBOARD AND WRAP WITH TAPE.

SUN BURSTS

Can you pop a balloon without touching it? Players discover the secret of doing this and make a big splash as well.

EQUIPMENT

A balloon for each player (Be sure to have extra balloons on hand.)
2 or 3 magnifying glasses
String

SITUATION

A wall or a fence on a sunny day

TIME

25 minutes

DIRECTIONS

1. Have each player inflate and tie a balloon. For added drama, have players fill balloons one-fourth full of water.
2. Divide the group into two teams. Teams attach their balloons to a wall or fence with string.
3. The two teams line up, facing their balloons. Players stand one behind the other.
4. Give the first player in each line a magnifying glass. The object of the game is to burn a hole in the balloons with the intense beam of light created by a magnified sun ray.
5. When the leader says "Go," the first players of each team begin to burn into the balloon. After a player breaks a balloon, he or she passes the magnifying glass to the next team member and runs to the end of the line.
6. The first team to break all its balloons is the winner and—naturally—receives a burst of applause.

LIGHT WRITE

This activity is light years behind laser technology, but the same basic principle applies.

EQUIPMENT

3 or 4 magnifying glasses to share
Paper for each player

SITUATION

Paved area on a sunny day

TIME

35 minutes

DIRECTIONS

1. Divide the group into smaller groups, each with its own magnifying glass. Give each player a sheet of paper.

2. Have players place their paper on the sidewalk or pavement. Place stones on each corner of the paper to keep it from blowing away.

3. Taking turns, players in each group hold the magnifying glass so that the sun shines through it and makes a dot of light on the paper. Keep adjusting the magnifying glass slowly until it makes the smallest and brightest dot possible. Hold the glass until the paper begins to burn. As the paper starts to scorch, players move the dot slowly to form their initial. This takes time, so be patient.

4. As players become proficient at making letters, have them try a collective drawing, each adding a line or dot.

5. Next, have teams or groups add letters to a single piece of paper. Passing it along, each player adds another scorched letter as the team tries to spell a word. The first team to complete a word in lightning time is the winner.

SUN BEAMS

In a city with tall glass buildings, you will probably see sun murals reflected off the windows of one building onto the shadowy side of another. At home, sun beams sneak inside and reflect off mirrors onto walls and ceilings. This activity will help players reflect on the sun's powers.

EQUIPMENT

Roll of aluminum foil
Hand mirrors
Make-up mirrors
Full-length mirrors
Mirrored mylar
Any reflecting materials
String
Scissors
Several wire coat hangers

SITUATION

A shadowy wall on a sunny day

TIME

40 minutes

DIRECTIONS

1. Find a shadowy wall with the sun directly behind it so that sunlight can be reflected back onto it.

2. Use a variety of reflecting materials. For example:

- Smooth pieces of foil create shimmering reflections.
- Round hand mirrors reflect sharp ovals and circles.
- Small make-up mirrors flash bright lines across walls.
- Large full-length mirrors reflect silhouettes of arms and legs.
- Mylar can be twisted and wiggled to reflect wavy shapes.

3. Have players work together to build one big light mural by arranging mirrors, foil, and mylar into one reflecting sculpture. Lean mirrors against chairs or prop them on tables, directing the beams of light into a reflective collage.

4. Use wire coat hangers and string to suspend foil and mylar. Cut pieces into shapes to make reflected stars, circles, and squiggles.

5. When the light sculpture is finished, players can add music, dancing and shaking arms and legs in front of mirrors to move reflections.

SNOW SHOWS

Here are some surprises that will warm up cold, snowy days. With these activities, players turn freshly fallen snow into their own play equipment.

SNOW HUNT

This hunt may seem like an archeological dig as players excavate the snow to find hidden objects.

EQUIPMENT

20 or 25 weatherproof objects (plastic blocks, containers, Frisbees, and so on)
A scoop for each player

SITUATION

An open yard just before a snowfall

TIME

20 minutes

DIRECTIONS

　1. Place the objects out in the playground during a snowfall. Leave them until they have been entirely covered by snow.
　2. Gather players at the edge of the yard and describe the hidden objects. With their scoops, players dig in the snow to find the objects.
　3. The player with the most discoveries is the winner.

BUTTON DOWN

This game is a variation on the traditional Button, Button, and requires not only a sharp eye but some warm gloves.

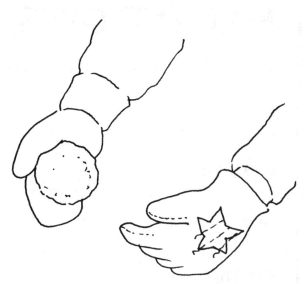

EQUIPMENT

A brightly colored button, coin, or pebble

SITUATION

Open playground with snow

TIME

15 minutes

DIRECTIONS

1. One player is chosen to be It. The rest of the group stands in a circle with the person who is It in the middle.

2. Players make four snowballs—one with a button, pebble, or coin hidden inside.

3. The person who is It says "Go," and everybody quickly passes the snowballs around the circle.

4. The person who is It counts to 25 and says "Button Down!" He or she then guesses which snowball has the button inside. Players holding snowballs break them open to see which one has the button. If the guess is correct, the player with the button is the next It. If the guess is wrong, he or she is It again for another round.

VARIATION

1. For a large group of 20 or more players, the game may be played the same way except that everyone makes a snowball, but only one has a button or pebble inside.

2. The person who is It counts to 25, says "Button Down," and has three guesses to find the button.

FOX AND GEESE

What better way to enjoy the snow and still keep warm?

EQUIPMENT

None

SITUATION

Freshly fallen snow on an open playground

TIME

20 minutes

DIRECTIONS

1. In the traditional game, players make a wheel-shaped design in the undisturbed snow. First, players walk in a circle, packing down a snow path and making the diameter as big as possible. Second, players make two intersecting paths, dividing the circle into four quarters (the amount of spokes may vary with the number of players). Where two paths cross in the center, stamp down an area of snow to make a safety zone.

2. In this variation, have players elaborate on the wheel design. Suggest doubling the design into a figure 8, quadruple it into a four leaf clover—or even create a Pac-Man maze!

3. To play, one player is selected to be the Fox and all the others are the Geese. During the chase, all the players must stay on the paths made in the snow.

4. When the leader says "Go," the Fox chases the Geese, trying to tag one of them. However, a Goose is immune from being tagged while standing in a safety zone. If another Goose comes along, the safety zone must be relinquished.

5. The first Goose to get caught by the Fox becomes the new Fox.

SNOWBALL SHOOTING RANGE

Get ready for a showdown as players show off their snowball sharpshooting skills.

EQUIPMENT

Tin cans, plastic containers, hula hoops—any nonbreakable object that can be used as a snowball target

SITUATION

Open playground after a fresh snowfall

TIME

20 minutes

DIRECTIONS

1. Divide the group into two teams.

2. Set up the shooting range on a table, fence, or wall. Suspend hula hoops from a tree and arrange cans and containers in a stack or across a table top.

3. Each team makes a pile of snowballs (two per player). Teams line up 5 to 10 yards away from the targets.

4. One player is selected to reset the objects. One by one, players take a turn throwing their snowballs. Each time an object is hit, his or her team gets a point. The team with the most points after every player has thrown is the winner.

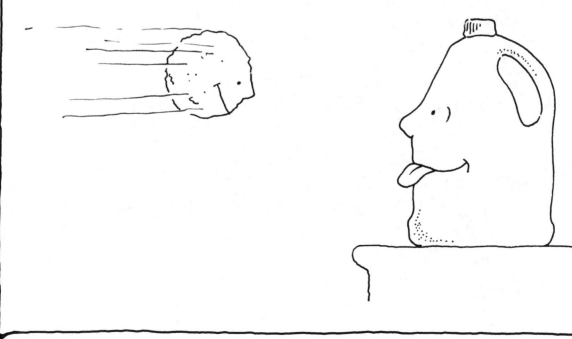

SNOW OFF

Admittedly, this game offers no clear-cut goal other than a well-organized excuse for being a little flaky.

EQUIPMENT

Watch

SITUATION

Freshly fallen snow

TIME

30 seconds

DIRECTIONS

1. Divide the group into two teams. This is a race against time, so it's important to have a player counting off or keeping track of seconds with a watch.

2. Mark a line in the snow between the two teams. The object of the game is to see who can pile the most snow on the other team's side of the line within 30 seconds.

3. When the leader says "Go," everyone picks up a handful of snow and tosses it across the line. Naturally this gets to be a little chaotic, but that's part of the game.

4. At the stroke of 30 seconds, the leader calls "Stop," and teams try to agree on the winner—if players have any energy left to make judgments.

SNOWBALL FOR ALL

The problem may seem simple, but the solution is a colossal challenge: How do you make a snowball big enough for an entire group to sit on? In this game the product is just as important as the process.

EQUIPMENT

None

SITUATION

Freshly fallen snow on an open playground

TIME

30 minutes

DIRECTIONS

1. After a snowfall, several players begin to roll a snowball. The object of the game is to make a gigantic snowball large enough for the whole group to sit on.

2. Everybody helps to roll the snowball. As it gets bigger and bigger, it gets harder to roll. Solving this problem will take some team work.

3. When the snowball can no longer budge, players line up ready to climb aboard. One by one, players carefully mount the snowball, helping each other balance without squashing it. The group wins when the last player is securely attached. If the whole group cannot fit on the snowball, try to beat this record after the next snowfall. In the meantime, colossal leftover snowballs are the perfect beginning for the world's largest snow sculpture.

VARIATION

1. Divide the group into two teams. Define a time limit of approximately three to five minutes.

2. The team that can roll the largest snowball topped with the most players is the winner.

SNOW BODIES

After snow has fallen, it's time to work fast to use this temporary gift and mold it into our own creations. Snow that is a bit moist works best.

EQUIPMENT

None

SITUATION

Open playground with moist snow

TIME

30 minutes

DIRECTIONS

1. Before taking the group outdoors, discuss some ideas for snow creatures. Depending on the ability of the group, snow sculptures can be as simple as a row of snowballs for a multi-segmented caterpillar to an intricately carved elephant from a big mound.

2. After players have gone outside, divide them into smaller groups of three or four. Each team decides on their own creature and begins to roll mounds of snow—big mounds for bodies and head, smaller mounds for tails and feet. Since snow is heavy, suggest that the weight of the sculpture be at the base and that legs and feet can be carved out later.

3. After a rough outline of snow has been created, sculptors begin to scoop away places for eyes, noses, arms, legs, tails, fins, and so forth. Sticks are good scooping tools.

4. To give snow creatures character, add twigs and sticks for arms, feet, or ears and stones for buttons, eyes, and teeth.

TWO-HEADED SNOW MONSTER

SNOW PORTRAITS

Portrait artists usually have their own special vision of their models. Whistler's mother didn't just sit around all day, and Mona Lisa probably had her grumpy moments. These snow portraits may be impossible to preserve in a museum, but art critics will still enjoy the opportunity to make their judgments.

EQUIPMENT

A piece of paper and a pencil for each player

SITUATION

Freshly fallen snow

TIME

30 minutes

SPRAY SCULPTURES LIGHTLY WITH WATER AND LET FREEZE FOR A SHINY SURFACE.

DIRECTIONS

 1. Give each player a small piece of paper and a pencil on which to write his or her name.

 2. Players fold their paper and drop it into a box or hat.

 3. One by one, players take turns picking names out of the box, making sure not to show whom they have chosen.

 4. Each player makes a snow portrait of the person he or she has selected. Portraits do not have to be exact representations but should try to capture some characteristics of the person.

 5. When snow artists have completed their portraits, have everyone take turns identifying the models.

ICE SCULPTURE

You've probably filled an ice cube tray with water, put it in the freezer—and presto chango—you've got frozen squares of water called ice cubes. If it's so easy to make cubes of ice, how about making other shapes?

EQUIPMENT

Rubber gloves, balloons, rubber bands, plastic buckets, plastic food containers, ice cube trays, and any other flexible containers
Rubber bands
Water

SITUATION

Freezing weather

TIME

30 minutes

DIRECTIONS

1. This project may be started indoors and taken outside.
2. The ice shape depends on the shape of the mold. For example:

- Make a hand-shaped ice sculpture by filling a rubber glove with water. Secure the open end with a rubber band. Prop the glove so that the water won't leak out and leave it outside overnight to freeze.
- Freeze water in a cake mold for a donut-shaped ice sculpture.
- Ice cube trays can become a new form of cubism by placing pennies, bottle caps, pebbles, or any other cube-sized object in each compartment. Fill with water and freeze. Seen through ice, shapes look altered.
- Blow up two or three small balloons and place them in a plastic bucket. Fill the bucket with water—holding the balloons in the water—and freeze. Carefully remove the ice and take out the balloons for a super shape.
- For a free-form sculpture, fill a balloon with water. Tie the open end securely and freeze. The shape of the unfrozen balloon can be changed by pinching it with rubber bands.

3. To unmold sculptures, run under warm water for a moment.
4. Ice sculptures melt quickly indoors but will last long enough to decorate a party. Those displayed outdoors will keep just as long as the temperature is below freezing.

SNOW PALACE

Winter wonderlands can have their own palace with this easy construction technique. Together, players will be able to build a home for the ruling monarch—but filling the job may have to be done democratically.

EQUIPMENT

7 to 10 bread pans or meatloaf pans

SITUATION

Snowy area

TIME

35 minutes

PACK SNOW IN PAN.

TURN OVER, TAP PAN, AND RELEASE SNOWBRICK.

DIRECTIONS

1. Divide the group into smaller groups of three.
2. Players discuss the design of the snow palace. Define the number of rooms and their shape—rectangular, circular, or square. Each group is responsible for a different area of the palace.
3. Give each group a bread pan or meatloaf pan. Players pack snow in the pan, turn it over, tap it, and release a molded snowbrick. This works best if the snow is a bit moist. Sprinkle a little water on very dry snow to make it more malleable.
4. Players continue to pile bricks, stacking them the long way for a stronger wall. Pack snow between bricks to make them solid.
5. Finish off the palace with a moat and a turret—and a reception in the snow ballroom.

AIR RITES

The sky's the limit as players get wind of these air crafts. The wind and sky offer players a chance to explore the universe without leaving the playground.

WIND WHIRLERS

Millions of light years ago, on a far away planet, extraterrestrial beings discovered that paper plates would fly when twirled in the air. This eventually led to the design of the first flying saucer. Now humans on this planet can play with the same basic material used by millions of space beings throughout the universe!

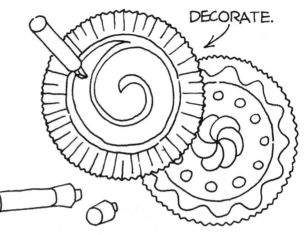

DECORATE.

EQUIPMENT

Paper plates (two per player)
Stapler to share
Felt markers in assorted colors

SITUATION

Large open area

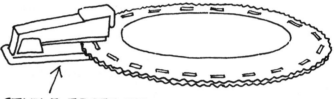

STAPLE TOGETHER.

TIME

25 minutes

DIRECTIONS

1. Divide the group into smaller groups of three or four players.
2. Give each player two paper plates and give each group a stapler and an assortment of felt markers.
3. Have players decorate plates with "extraterrestrial" designs such as flashes of light, swirls, zips, and zaps. Spirals look great as spinning saucers whirl through the sky. Use permanent markers so colors don't run if the plates get wet.
4. To construct the whirlers, each player staples two plates together, either back to back or front to front. Back-to-back whirlers dip and curve while front-to-front whirlers tend to fly faster and straighter.
5. After some individual whirler experimentation, players might want to try additional modifications, such as cutting holes in the center or adding other paper elements, to see how they affect flight patterns.

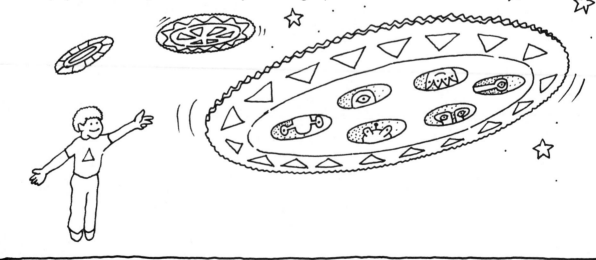

PARATROOPERS

Parachutes have given people a new view of the world. Now here's a new view of parachutes.

EQUIPMENT

12″ square of cloth for each player (a handkerchief or plastic trash bag can be substituted)
Five 12″ pieces of string for each player
Scissors to share
Wooden clothespin or spool for each player
Felt markers in assorted colors

SITUATION

A windy day in an open area

TIME

35 minutes

DIRECTIONS

1. Give each player a wooden clothespin or empty spool, a 12-inch square of cloth or plastic, and five 12-inch pieces of string.

2. Pinch the corners of the cloth and tie a string to each corner.

3. For players using clothespins, tie all four corner strings together; at the knot, attach a separate piece of string; finally, tie around the top of the clothespin with the added string. For those with spools, thread all four strings through the hole and tie them together into a knot so that the spool does not slip off. Use felt markers to decorate clothespins and spools with faces, goggles, and jumpsuits.

4. When chutes have been constructed, paratroopers are ready for some basic training. Designate a spot in the middle of the playground and mark it with a piece of chalk or a stone.

5. Paratroopers line up ready to launch. Roll parachutes up around spools or clothespins before throwing. On the count of three, paratroopers toss their chutes into the air with an underhand throw. The paratrooper whose chute floats closest to the target is a super-duper-trooper.

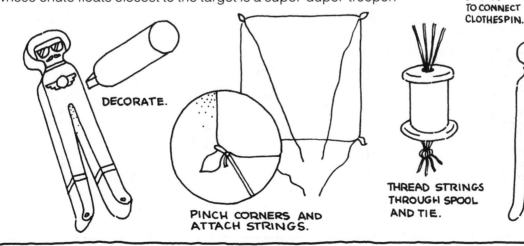

DECORATE.

PINCH CORNERS AND ATTACH STRINGS.

THREAD STRINGS THROUGH SPOOL AND TIE.

ATTACH A SEPARATE STRING TO CONNECT CLOTHESPIN.

CROSS-COUNTRY FLYING CONTEST

It seems that everyone has a favorite paper plane to fly. In this game, players test their best models against all others in a long-distance flight to the finish.

EQUIPMENT

A sheet of construction paper for each player
Paper clips
Chalk or piece of rope

SITUATION

Large open field or yard

TIME

25 minutes

DIRECTIONS

1. Give each player a piece of construction paper. Construction paper is heavier than most paper and gives planes extra weight to stabilize flights on a windy day.

2. Each player folds his or her paper into a glider. To keep planes aloft longer, suggest that players give gliders as much wing span as possible.

3. After planes have been folded, players are ready to test them. If planes flutter or swoop, try adding a paper clip to the front of the body. The added weight of the clip helps the plane push through the air more smoothly and easily.

4. When all pilots are ready, it is time to begin the race. On an open playground, field, yard, or parking lot, designate start and finish lines with chalk or a line of rope.

5. To begin, players line up with their planes. When the leader says "Go," everyone launches the planes. Players dash to where planes have landed and launch again. This continues until one player crosses the finish line.

THE QUINTESSENTIAL PINWHEEL

For years, the pinwheel has been neglected, leaving its potential almost totally unexplored—until now. These instructions will help make a single pinwheel that will prepare you for the wonderful variations.

EQUIPMENT

A square of construction paper, 5″ or 6″ on each side
Pencil
Ruler
Scissors
Tape
Straight pin, pushpin, or thumbtack
Dowel

SITUATION

Flat surface

TIME

15 minutes

DIRECTIONS

1. With a pencil and ruler, draw straight lines diagonally from corner to corner on the square of construction paper.

2. Cut in on the lines from each corner approximately two-thirds of the way to the center.

3. Curl each corner in toward the center and tape down.

4. To complete the pinwheel, push a thumbtack or straight pin through the center where all the corners come together. Stick the pin into a dowel or thin cardboard tube. Give the pinwheel a few turns to get it started and let the wind do the rest.

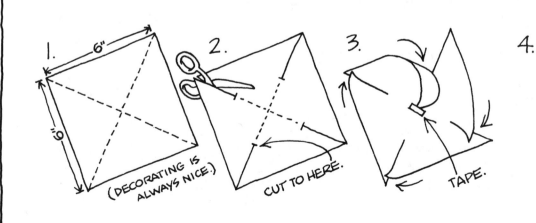

TWIRLING TREES

Famous architect Mies van der Rohe once said, "Less is more," but I prefer the saying, "The more the merrier," but then again, Mies never built quite like this—more or less.

EQUIPMENT

¼" dowels or thin cardboard tubes, 36" long (3 or 4 for each player)
Masking tape to share
Twine to share
Pinwheel supplies (see Pinwheel, page 33)

SITUATION

A flat surface on a breezy day

TIME

35 minutes

DIRECTIONS

1. Groups of 8 or 10 are easy to organize so that players can make individual "Trees." Larger groups can be divided into smaller teams of three or four with each team constructing one Tree together.

2. Players may prefer working on the ground or at a table. Divide supplies—paper, scissors, pencils, rulers, tape, string, dowels or tubes, and pins—evenly between players or teams.

3. To make a tree structure, use a 36-inch dowel for the trunk. Mark dowel every 6 inches.

4. Cut a series of dowels into progressively smaller sizes—36 inches, 27 inches, 18 inches, and 9 inches.

5. Players attach a smaller crosspiece of dowel to the trunk every 6 inches. Individual designers can shape their Tree using different sizes of cross dowels. Lash pieces together by wrapping string or tape around intersecting dowels.

6. Make as many pinwheels as you need to fill each tree frame. Attach pinwheels to tree with pins, staggering them so they do not bump into each other while spinning.

7. Completed Trees may be used in parades, to decorate dull play spaces, or may be combined for a spinning spectacle.

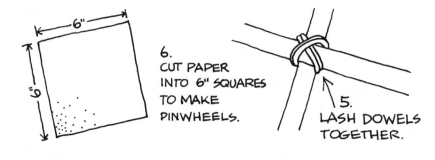

6.
CUT PAPER INTO 6" SQUARES TO MAKE PINWHEELS.

5.
LASH DOWELS TOGETHER.

MOBILE UNITS

Mobiles are hanging sculptures that change shape as they move in the wind. In this project, we add movement to movement by adding pinwheels.

EQUIPMENT

Dowels, balsa sticks, or thin cardboard tubes
   from clothes hangers—8 to 10 per mobile
String
Pinwheel supplies (see Pinwheel, page 33)

SITUATION

Flat surface for construction

TIME

30 minutes

DIRECTIONS

1. Have players make as many pinwheels as they like. Six to ten is good for this project. If supplies are limited and the group is large, have two or three players work together on a single mobile.

2. After pinwheels have been constructed, attach them to the ends of dowels, balsa sticks, or to the sides of hollow cardboard tubes (like those from clothes hangers).

3. Suspend sticks from string, carefully balancing them by moving the string back and forth until the sticks are horizontal.

4. Hang mobiles from a branch, overhang, or any place it can be mobilized in the wind.

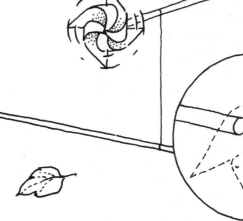

PROP TOPS

These propellers will keep heads spinning.

EQUIPMENT

1½" x 22" strip of construction paper for each
   player
2 balsa sticks, plastic straws, or thin cardboard
   tubes from clothes hangers for each player
Pinwheel supplies (see Pinwheel, page 33)
Masking tape to share
Staplers to share
Scissors to share

SITUATION

Flat surface on a windy day

TIME

30 minutes

DIRECTIONS

  1. Give each player two balsa sticks, drinking straws, or cardboard
tubes from clothes hangers, a strip of 1½- by 22-inch paper, and pinwheel
supplies.

  2. Each player wraps the long strip of paper around his or her head.
Tape headbands with help from another player. To reinforce, slip off
headbands and staple together. Trim excess.

  3. Players make two pinwheels and attach them to two sticks or tubes
with pins.

  4. Attach sticks to both sides of the headband with tape.

  5. Place Prop Tops on the head and take them out for a spin—the faster
players move, the faster the Prop Tops turn.

DECORATE HEADBANDS.

WRAP HEADBANDS AROUND HEADS AND TAPE.

ATTACH PINWHEELS TO DOWELS.

TAPE DOWEL INSIDE BAND OR CUT 2 SLITS AND SLIP DOWEL THROUGH.

WHEELS ON WHEELS

If you've ever tried sticking a pinwheel out the window of a moving car, you know that the passing air currents make it spin like crazy. Pinwheels on your moving bike won't make it fly, but they will transform it into a moving mobile.

ATTACH PINWHEELS TO DOWEL.

EQUIPMENT

An 18″ dowel, balsa stick, or thin cardboard tube from a clothes hanger for each player
Pinwheel supplies (see Pinwheel, page 33)

TIE DOWEL TO FRONT OF HANDLEBARS.

SITUATION

Flat surface for construction and a bike

TIME

25 minutes

DIRECTIONS

1. Each player is given a dowel, balsa stick, or thin cardboard tube that is about 18 inches long.
2. Players make three pinwheels and attach them, spaced evenly, across the dowel.
3. Tie the dowel across the front of the handlebars by wrapping string or tape around it securely.
4. Ride the bike and watch the pinwheels spin.

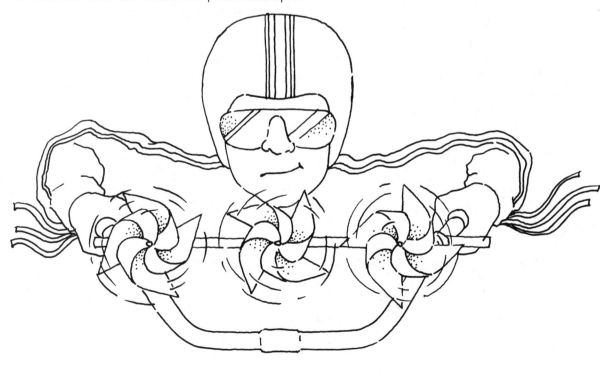

BUBBLE BASICS

Traditional bubble blowing is guaranteed fun, but these fancy soap structures are a delight. Surprisingly, no fancy equipment is needed—just things found in almost any kitchen.

EQUIPMENT

Several rectangular pans—dish pans, shallow
   trays, or baking sheets
Large plastic container with top—bleach bottle or
   milk container
Dishwashing soap
Glycerine (may be found in any drugstore)
Plastic drinking straws
Several large juice or coffee cans
String
Roll of electrical tape

SITUATION

Flat surface (picnic table) in an open area

TIME

45 minutes

DIRECTIONS

   1. Bubbles can be as messy as they are fun, so find a place you don't mind getting wet. Set up a table and place the rectangular pans on it so that they are ready to be filled with the soap solution.

   2. To make the soap solution, fill a clean plastic container with a quart of warm water and mix in about eight tablespoons of soap. The higher priced dishwashing soaps seem to make the strongest bubbles. To give bubbles more elasticity, add six to eight tablespoons of glycerine to the mixture. Shake well and pour into the pans.

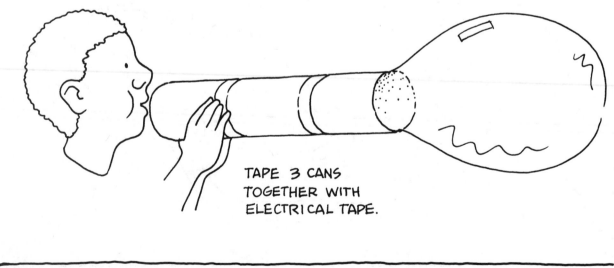

3. The tube is the basic bubble-blowing tool. Plastic drinking straws, tin cans (open at both ends), and wire coat hangers (stretched into a circular shape) are bubble blowers that might be handy. Experiment with different objects, such as disposable cups, to find undiscovered launchers.

4. Demonstrate bubble making by taking a drinking straw, dipping it into the soap solution, and getting a film across the end. Hold the straw over the surface of the solution and gently blow to form a bubble dome on the surface. Pull the straw out carefully. Next, blow another bubble dome, but this time leave the straw inserted and blow another bubble within the bubble.

5. Drinking straws work well as mini-bubble blowers. Tape several together in a group, dip into the solution, and blow a cluster of miniature bubbles.

6. To make really big bubbles, tape three tin cans together into a long tube something like an oversized straw. Use electrical tape because it's sticky and water resistant. The longer the tube, the smoother the flow of air and the less likely the bubble will break. Begin by blowing a large dome on the surface of the soap solution. Next, try making a free-floating bubble. Dip the end of the can into the solution to form a film across the end. Blow to make the film stretch into a long sausage-shaped bubble. To release, twist the tube to close off the bubble.

7. Another simple contraption for making gigantic bubbles can be made with two plastic drinking straws and a yard of string. Thread the string through both straws and tie the ends together. Hold the straws in each hand to create a rectangular frame. Place the frame into the soap solution. Lift carefully to stretch the film across it. With arms extended, pull the frame upward. The air pressure will form a bubble. To release the bubble, bring the straws together and swing up. It takes a little practice to master these fancy bubbles.

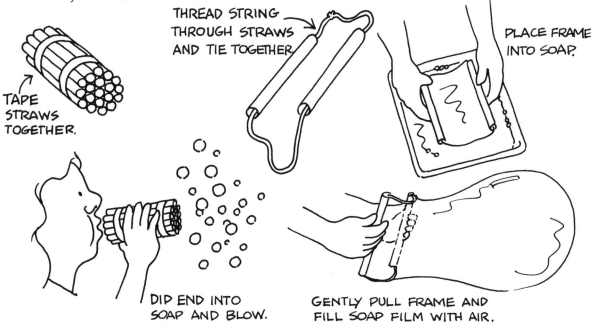

TAPE STRAWS TOGETHER.

THREAD STRING THROUGH STRAWS AND TIE TOGETHER.

PLACE FRAME INTO SOAP.

DIP END INTO SOAP AND BLOW.

GENTLY PULL FRAME AND FILL SOAP FILM WITH AIR.

BUBBLE SCULPTURE

After trying bubble basics, players are ready for the art of bubble making. The idea is to see how many different shapes can be made with the fragile spheres. These suggestions will start imaginations bubbling.

BLOW BUBBLE ON THE BOTTOM OF INVERTED CAN.

TURN OVER AND ATTACH BUBBLE TO BUBBLE.

EQUIPMENT

Soap solution (see Bubble Basics, pages 38–39)
Several large juice or coffee cans
Box of drinking straws
Paper clips

SITUATION

Flat surface (picnic table) in an open area

TIME

45 minutes

DIRECTIONS

Bubbles can be blown on top of, between, and inside of objects. In this project, experimentation is encouraged. Allow players to invent their own bubble sculptures using the following techniques as their foundation. To begin, set up the soap solution in trays.

Bubble Chains

   1. With a solution-filled straw, blow a bubble dome on the unopened end of a juice can.
   2. Pick the can up and invert it with the bubble hanging underneath.
   3. Dip the straw in the solution and attach another bubble by placing the straw next to the bottom of the first bubble. Then blow.
   4. Add as many bubbles as possible to the bubble chain.
   5. Create a bubble column by attaching the bottom of the chain to a wet soapy tray.

ATTACH THE LAST BUBBLE TO THE SOAP SOLUTION.

STRAWS AND EXTRA·LONG STRING

Bubble Trouble

1. This enormous task takes the coordinated effort of two players. A pair of players makes a giant straw and string frame, 6 to 10 feet long (see Bubble Basics, pages 38–39).

2. Run the frame through the solution very slowly, carefully filling it with a film of soapy liquid.

3. Gently stretch the frame out. Although a bubble this size will not be able to snap free, the film will expand and stretch into an undulating soapy shape. Watch what happens when a bubble that size breaks.

Double Bubble

1. An enormous bubble can be made by two players blowing a bubble together with tin can blowers. On a soapy surface, two players begin blowing two separate bubbles, trying to connect them into one single bubble. Invite other players to add their bubbles, with all players slowly filling their shared dome with air.

2. Next, have two players try making a free-floating Double Bubble by blowing their bubbles together through their tin cans. When both bubbles are connected into one big bubble, players release their end one at a time by twisting off their cans.

Geometric Bubble

1. Did you ever see a square bubble? Players can make bubbles into cubes and pyramids with the help of a drinking straw frame. To make a frame, connect straws together with paper clips by slipping one clip curl into one straw and the other into another. (see illustration).

2. Geometric bubbles aren't blown; instead, soap film fills the sides of the frame to create the shape. Players dip frames into the soap solution until all the sides are filled.

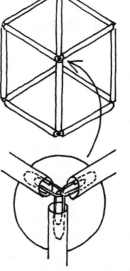

CONNECT STRAWS WITH PAPERCLIP CORNERS.

DIP EACH SIDE INTO SOAP SOLUTION.

BUBBLE OVER

Bubbles are very unpredictable. Just as things seem to be pleasantly floating along—pop!—there you are back where you started.

EQUIPMENT

2 pans of soap solution (see Bubble Basics, pages 38–39)
2 tin can bubble-blowing devices

SITUATION

Open area

TIME

10 minutes

DIRECTIONS

   1. The group is divided into two teams. Each team has a pan of soapy solution and a tin can bubble-blowing device. A person on each team is selected as the bubble blower.

   2. Mark the start and finish lines about 5 or 6 yards apart.

   3. Behind the starting line, each team huddles around their bubble blower. When the leader says "Go," the bubble blower blows a bubble. Team members must blow or fan their bubble across the playground to the finish line.

   4. If a bubble pops, team members must go back to the bubble blower at the start line and begin again.

   5. The first team to get its bubble over the finish line is the champion bubble-blowing team.

VARIATION

   1. Have teams meet in the middle of the playing field with goal lines indicated at either end.

   2. When the leader says "Go," a single bubble is blown.

   3. If a bubble pops, team members return to the start line and begin again.

   4. Each team tries to fan it across its goal line. The first team to do it is the winner.

SPINNERS

Cowhands spin lassos. Chinese dancers spin long pieces of fabric during celebrations and festivals. It's a spectacular but simple theatrical device that can be performed on any playground.

EQUIPMENT

A small wooden rectangle for each player, approximately 2″ x 1″ x ½″ (several pieces of corrugated cardboard laminated together can also work)
Drill with a ⅛″ bit
Staple gun
Twine or heavy string
Several rolls of different colors of crepe paper

SITUATION

Open area

TIME

25 minutes

DIRECTIONS

1. Prepare a piece of wood, approximately 2 inches by 1 inch by ½ inch, for each player. Drill a ⅛-inch hole at one end of each piece.

2. Give each player a piece of wood with a hole, a yard of twine, and several strands of crepe paper in various colors.

3. Players loop and tie the twine through the hole. On the opposite end, fasten a few strands of crepe paper with a stapler.

4. To play, swing the string and spin the piece of wood and crepe paper in a circular motion. Players will be immediately motivated to try variations on their own. Suggest a figure 8 motion, swinging the spinner in front, behind, and to the side of the player. Make sure that each player's spinner does not interfere with another player's spinner.

5. Gather everyone together for a group spinning circle or organize a spinning parade.

1. DRILL HOLE.

3. ATTACH STRING.

STAPLE ON STRANDS OF CREPE PAPER.

FULL-BLOWN COSTUMES

Players can blow up while wearing this breezy apparel.

EQUIPMENT

Lengths of 36"-wide fabric, old sheets, fabric
    scraps, large plastic trash bags, any other
    lightweight material
Stapler
Felt-tipped markers in assorted colors
Masking tape
String
Scissors to share

SITUATION

Open area on a windy day

TIME

30 minutes

DIRECTIONS

1. Give players a variety of old fabric that can be cut easily and will blow in the wind. Players share scissors, felt-tipped markers, tape, string, and staplers.

2. Before actually designing wind costumes, have players experiment with catching the wind in a piece of fabric. Two players hold either end of a long piece of fabric and run into the wind until it inflates.

3. Gather players together and suggest some design ideas. Players might attach wings to arms by looping fabric, stapling it and cutting a slit of fabric to slide arms through. Attach long ribbons or crepe paper to a strip of fabric and hold the end letting the ribbons stream along in the air. Taking some inspiration from colorful birds and butterflies, players may want to decorate their costumes with felt-tipped markers.

4. When costumes are completed, have players run across and around the playground to create the world's first human wind sculpture.

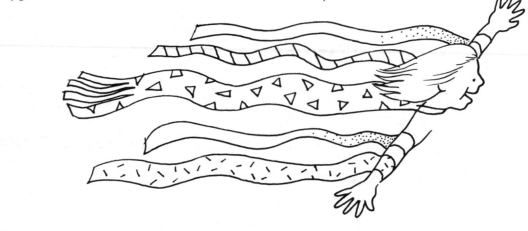

CHIME OUT

Turn a breeze into music with this charming chime.

EQUIPMENT

Plastic container (the kind that bread crumbs or sour cream come in) or a small cardboard box (a shoe box or smaller)
Heavy string, one 2′ length and numerous 10″ lengths per player
Scissors to share
Masking tape
An assortment of small metal bits (nails, screws, bottle caps, metal lids, and so forth)

SITUATION

A windy day

TIME

35 minutes

DIRECTIONS

1. Give each player a 16-ounce plastic food container (the kind bread crumbs, margarine, or sour cream come in) or a small box (such as a shoe box or small gift box). Players share string, tape, scissors, and an assortment of small metal bits such as lids, nails, bottle caps, and screws. Have players collect bits in advance.

2. To make the basic structure, poke four holes into the bottom of the container or box and thread a piece of 2-foot string in and out of the holes. Tie the ends together and hang from a branch.

3. Poke holes around the open edge of the container. Cut a 10-inch piece of string for each hole and tie.

4. Tape or tie small metal bits to the end of each string. Balance items so that the weight is even and the bits hit each other.

5. Let the wind chime hang in a tree or outside a window and let the wind do the rest.

FLIGHT PATTERNS

Get ready for an instant festival with these colorful clothesline banners. After you've hung the basic structure, you'll be surprised to see the year-round effect on young artists who will be able to fill the sky with visions from their heads.

EQUIPMENT

2 pulleys
2 hooks
50′ to 100′ of nylon rope (double the size of the
   area spanned)
Rope fasteners
Assorted fabric scraps—ribbons, felt pieces, and
   so forth
Lengths of fabric
Rolls of paper—adding machine paper, brown
   wrapping paper, and so forth
Tempera paint in assorted colors
Brushes
Staplers
Scissors
2 to 4 dozen clothespins

SITUATION

The air space between a building and a pole or tree

TIME

60 minutes to hang the clothesline structure
45 minutes to decorate the clothesline

DIRECTIONS

The Clothesline Structure

1. Depending on the size of the group and the space available, suspend one or two clotheslines over the playground. Clotheslines should be hung as high as possible and may be run diagonally from ground level to the top of a tree or across the playground from a second-story window. For each clothesline, you'll need to go to a hardware store and buy two pulleys, two hooks to attach the pulleys, 50 to 100 feet of nylon rope (measure the length of the space and double it), and one rope fastener.

2. After clotheslines are hung, players are ready to fill them with banners and murals.

The Banners

1. Banners can be made from fabric scraps, long lengths of fabric, and long rolls of paper. Cut fabric or paper into whimsical shapes such as crescents, free forms, and zigzags. Cloth banners can be sewn together, but for temporary flyers try stapling and pinning designs. Paper banners won't withstand the rain, but they are fun for the day. Simply paint designs with tempera paint onto long rolls of wrapping paper or thin adding machine paper.

2. When banners are completed, clip them to ropes with clothespins and hoist away! Change the space by moving the banners across the playground. Add more and more banners to make a gigantic group wind sculpture.

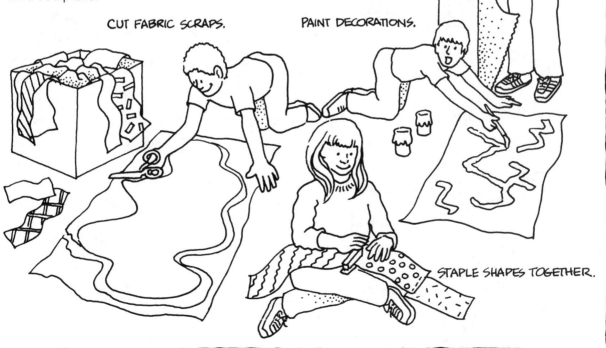

CUT FABRIC SCRAPS.

PAINT DECORATIONS.

STAPLE SHAPES TOGETHER.

FLYING FANTASIES

In 1943, Dr. Francis Rogallo introduced a breakthrough in kite design that spawned hang gliders and flying waterskiers. Frank Scott, inspired by Rogallo, designed one of the most reliable kites ever—the sled kite. This kite is simple to make and easy to fly. It's the perfect kite to get our fantasies off the ground.

EQUIPMENT

A white plastic trash bag, 20 or 30 gallons, for each player
Three 24" dowels, balsa sticks, or thin strips of cardboard for each player
Scissors to share
Felt-tipped markers in assorted colors
Masking tape
A large ball of string, enough for an 80" length and some flying string per player

SITUATION

Large open area on a windy day

TIME

45 minutes

DIRECTIONS

1. Give each player a white plastic trash bag and three 24-inch dowels or balsa sticks. Players can share tape, scissors, markers, and the ball of string.

2. Cut trash bags apart and lay out flat.

3. Draw a pattern (see illustration). The kite may be bigger or smaller but should use these proportions.

4. Lay dowels across the bag (see illustration) and attach with tape.

5. Fold tape around the corners to be tied. Punch a hole to tie the string and loop a long piece, about 80 inches, from hole to hole.

6. Attach a flying string to the looped string.

7. Have players suggest ideas for flying fantasies—a face in the clouds, a hovering UFO, a flying pickle, an eye in the sky, or a pie in the sky. Draw decorations with felt markers.

8. To launch, face the wind and run slowly until the wind catches the kite. Let the kite up a little at a time. Runners should look where they are going and watch out for fantasy-eating trees!

VARIATION

To stabilize kites and to keep them facing the right direction, add a tail. Tails are usually four times the length of the kite and should be made of lightweight material attached to a string such as tissue paper, crepe paper, or paper napkins. Attach paper by pinching a square of paper in the center and twisting like a bow or cutting a square into triangular flags. Staple around a piece of string and attach to the bottom of the kite.

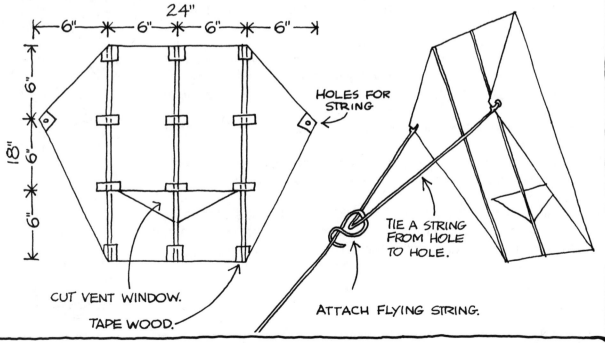

CUT VENT WINDOW.

TAPE WOOD.

HOLES FOR STRING

TIE A STRING FROM HOLE TO HOLE.

ATTACH FLYING STRING.

SKY SCULPTURE

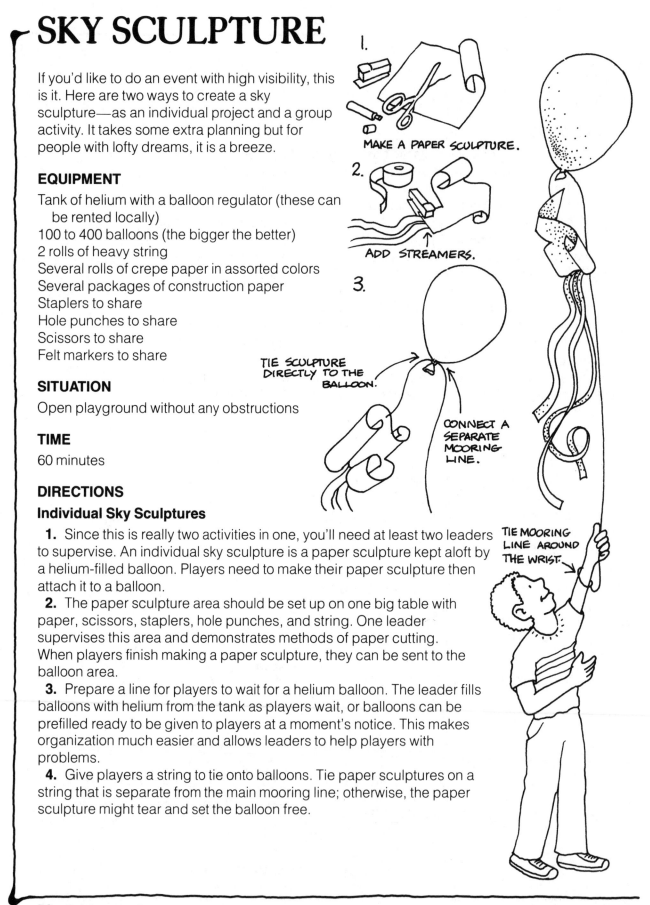

1. MAKE A PAPER SCULPTURE.

2. ADD STREAMERS.

3. TIE SCULPTURE DIRECTLY TO THE BALLOON.

CONNECT A SEPARATE MOORING LINE.

TIE MOORING LINE AROUND THE WRIST.

If you'd like to do an event with high visibility, this is it. Here are two ways to create a sky sculpture—as an individual project and a group activity. It takes some extra planning but for people with lofty dreams, it is a breeze.

EQUIPMENT

Tank of helium with a balloon regulator (these can be rented locally)
100 to 400 balloons (the bigger the better)
2 rolls of heavy string
Several rolls of crepe paper in assorted colors
Several packages of construction paper
Staplers to share
Hole punches to share
Scissors to share
Felt markers to share

SITUATION

Open playground without any obstructions

TIME

60 minutes

DIRECTIONS

Individual Sky Sculptures

1. Since this is really two activities in one, you'll need at least two leaders to supervise. An individual sky sculpture is a paper sculpture kept aloft by a helium-filled balloon. Players need to make their paper sculpture then attach it to a balloon.

2. The paper sculpture area should be set up on one big table with paper, scissors, staplers, hole punches, and string. One leader supervises this area and demonstrates methods of paper cutting. When players finish making a paper sculpture, they can be sent to the balloon area.

3. Prepare a line for players to wait for a helium balloon. The leader fills balloons with helium from the tank as players wait, or balloons can be prefilled ready to be given to players at a moment's notice. This makes organization much easier and allows leaders to help players with problems.

4. Give players a string to tie onto balloons. Tie paper sculptures on a string that is separate from the main mooring line; otherwise, the paper sculpture might tear and set the balloon free.

Group Sky Sculpture

1. The setup for a large group is about the same as it is for individuals except that everyone is working on the same big sculpture. Run a long cord between two poles or trees on which balloons can be tied.

2. Individual players get balloons from a person at the helium tank and tie them directly to the cord. As more and more balloons are attached, the cord will be transformed into a colorful arch.

3. While players keep filling the cord with balloons, other players begin to attach paper sculptures and crepe paper. Pieces of paper can be filled with felt marker designs, poems, names, and other drawings.

4. When the sculpture looks filled and there are no more balloons to attach, announce the launching parade. Have players hold the cord and cut the ends free. March with the sculpture through the playground, around the sidewalks, and out to a wide-open launching space. Count down with players, release it—and blast off!

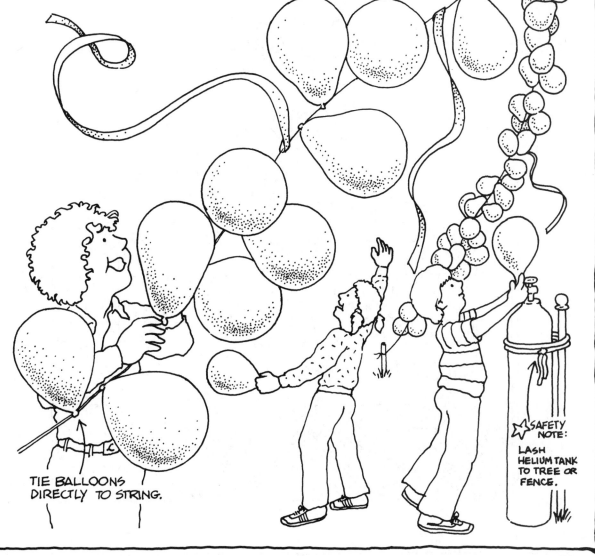

ADD CREPE PAPER STRANDS.

TIE BALLOONS DIRECTLY TO STRING.

SAFETY NOTE:

LASH HELIUM TANK TO TREE OR FENCE.

TIGHT SPOTS

Fun can be found anywhere. These group games and creative activities are played in limited or unusual spaces.

MOUSE TRAP

These mischievous mice tiptoe through a treacherous trap so as not to disturb the drowsy feline from a cat nap.

EQUIPMENT

None

SITUATION

Small area

TIME

10 minutes

DIRECTIONS

1. Four or five players are chosen to be the Trap and form a circle by holding hands. Arms are raised to create entrances and exits to and from the Trap.

2. One person is chosen to be the Cat. The Cat faces away from the Trap with eyes closed, as if asleep.

3. The rest of the players are the Mice. As the game begins, the Mice walk in and out of the Trap trying to get the cheese past the sleepy Cat.

4. The Cat, just pretending to be asleep, suddenly opens his or her eyes and yells "Snap!" The players forming the Trap bring down their arms and capture whoever may be in the circle. The Mice captured become part of the Trap.

5. As the game continues, the Trap becomes larger until all but one Mouse is caught. The victorious Mouse gets a Swiss Cheese Cheer!

VOLCANO

Playgrounds will erupt into a good time as players let off steam in this explosive activity.

EQUIPMENT

None

SITUATION

Open area

TIME

10 minutes

DIRECTIONS

   1. A player is selected to be It. The rest of the players are divided into two groups. The two groups form a double circle, one within the other.
   2. Each player in the outer circle stands behind a player in the inner circle. The inner circle is the volcano. The person who is It stands in the center ready to erupt.
   3. When the person who is It calls "Volcano!" the players standing around the volcano in the outer circle begin to panic and run around changing places with one another. Meanwhile, the person who is It and the players standing in the inner circle start the lava flowing by clapping their hands.
   4. Outer players continue to switch places while the inner players clap. When the person who is It stops clapping, the players standing in the inner circle stop also.
   5. Everyone in the outer circle and the person who is It rushes to find a spot behind one of the players from the inner circle. The player left without a spot is the next erupting It.

SCRABBLE SCRAMBLE

Players will be literally spellbound as they scramble to be letter-perfect.

EQUIPMENT

31 sheets of construction or typing paper for
  each team
Black felt marker

SITUATION

Open area

TIME

15 minutes

DIRECTIONS

  1. Make two sets of alphabet cards with paper and marker. Print one large letter on each sheet. Give each set two sheets of A, E, I, O, and U.
  2. Divide the group into two teams. Teams line up at one end of the playground, and the two lettered stacks are placed on the opposite end about 10 yards away.
  3. The leader calls out a category—sports, TV, fast food, birds, trees, and so forth. Teams huddle together to agree on a word to spell that relates to the category. For example, if the category is "Tree," one team might spell "Maple" and the other "Elm."
  4. Teams run to their alphabet stacks and scramble to find the necessary letters. Team members grab letters and run back, arranging themselves in the proper order.
  5. The first team to spell a word receives a point for each letter. The team with the most points after a predetermined number of rounds is the winner.

MERRILY-GO-ROUND

Carved carousels are beautiful examples of folk
art. In this case, folks become a beautiful
merry-go-round.

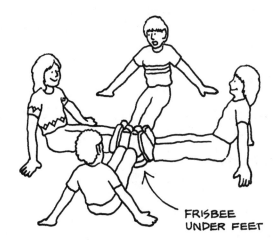

FRISBEE
UNDER FEET

EQUIPMENT

A Frisbee or an inverted trash can cover for each
  group

SITUATION

Open grassy area

TIME

15 minutes

DIRECTIONS

  1. Divide the group into teams of eight players.
  2. Four players sit in a circle with legs extended and feet in the middle.
Two of the facing players press their feet together and rest them on an
inverted Frisbee or trash can cover. The two other players place their feet
against either side of the first players' feet to create a tight bond.
  3. Four more players stand between the four seated players and form a
double wrist grasp with players seated on either side.
  4. On the word "Lift," the standing players take a small step back, and
the sitting players lift their hips from the ground, keeping their knees and
backs straight.
  5. Standing players move around to their left while the sitting people
pivot on the moving Frisbee. As in traditional carousel band organs,
players might like to sing some old-time favorites like "Yankee Doodle" or
"Row, Row, Row Your Boat."

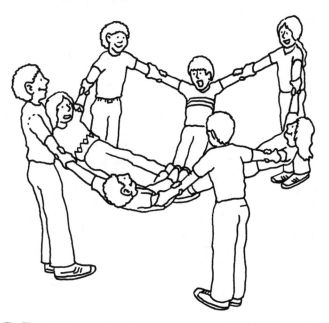

WATER BRIGADE

Water will be pouring, but players won't need to grab an umbrella for this water race to the last drop.

EQUIPMENT

4 buckets
A disposable cup (styrofoam or paper) for each
    player

SITUATION

Long narrow open area

TIME

15 minutes

DIRECTIONS

1. Divide the group into two teams. Teams stand in two parallel lines.
2. Place a bucket at either end of each team. Fill the buckets at one end of each team with water while the buckets on the opposite ends remain empty.
3. Give each player a disposable cup. The object of the game is for each team to transfer the water from the filled bucket—cup by cup—to the empty bucket.
4. When the leader says "Go," the first players on each team dip their cups into their buckets. The water is passed from player to player on each team by pouring it into the next cup. The last players pour their cups into the empty bucket.
5. The winning team is the one that finishes first with the most water. A fast team may fill its bucket first but might meet its Waterloo if a portion of the water is carelessly spilled along the way.

JUST IN PASSING

Games don't necessarily need to be competitive or have a specific goal in order to be fun. The simple act of passing a ball encourages players to add their own variations—inventing the game as they go along.

EQUIPMENT

6 to 8 balls (basketballs, beach balls, or Nerf balls are best)

SITUATION

Open area

TIME

15 minutes

DIRECTIONS

1. Have players stand in a circle.
2. Begin by passing a ball around the circle in one direction. Try passing the ball over head, through legs, and around backs. Get a rhythm going. Players may want to chant "Pass, pass, pass" so that the ball keeps moving as fast as possible.
3. As players master a one-way pass, heighten the challenge by passing another ball in the opposite direction. This will cause some silly confusion but insist that balls keep moving no matter what. You can also yell "Switch!" and have players reverse the directions in which they are passing the two balls.
4. To keep things exciting, keep adding more balls so that players haven't time to think. Eventually the game will end in one big free-for-all ball.

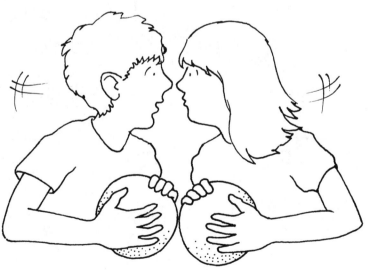

ROPE RING

Not even Ringling Brothers can match this one-ring circus.

EQUIPMENT

Approximately 50 feet of clothesline rope

SITUATION

Open area

TIME

20 minutes

DIRECTIONS

1. Tie the ends of the rope together to make a circle.
2. Players stand outside the rope in a circle, holding it with both hands.
3. One player is selected to be the Ringmaster and to stand in the middle. The Ringmaster tries to tap the hand of a ringside player holding the rope.
4. Players can drop the rope to avoid being tapped. The Ringmaster may try to trick players by pretending to tap one player and then tap another.
5. When a player is tapped while holding the rope, he or she becomes the next Ringmaster, and the thrills and chills continue.

VARIATION

For large groups, two or three Ringmasters will keep players off-guard and the show more exciting.

LEAN-TOO

The motto of this mutually supportive game may
be "Lean and Let Lean."

EQUIPMENT

None

SITUATION

Small open area

TIME

10 minutes

DIRECTIONS

1. Players stand in a circle, join hands, and count off alternately by ones and twos.

2. Keeping backs and legs as straight as possible, players who are "ones" lean forward toward the middle of the circle while all the "twos" lean backward toward the outside. Players counterbalance each other for support.

3. Once the group has gotten its balance, slowly reverse leaners—the "ones" lean backward and the "twos" lean forward. Have players see how smoothly they can alternate.

4. After players have leaned in and out, have everyone try stepping to the right or left moving around in a circle. There are only winners in this turning circle of slanted players.

PEANUT BUTTER AND JELLY

Someone in the group is destined to become the world's most popular combination.

EQUIPMENT

2 balls (beach balls or Nerf balls work best)

SITUATION

Open area

TIME

10 minutes

DIRECTIONS

1. The group stands in a circle.
2. Players pass one of the balls, "Peanut Butter," around the circle.
3. To make things sticky, the second ball, "Jelly," is tossed from player to player in any direction. Players must keep both balls moving without stopping. The object of the game is for the Jelly to catch up with the Peanut Butter.
4. When one player catches both balls, everyone shouts "Peanut butter and jelly!" Then everyone starts again.

VARIATION

For a more competitive game, change the names of the balls to "Over" and "Out." Players pass the balls but try to avoid catching them both. When one player happens to catch both at once, everyone shouts "Over and out!" That player is then out of the game.

YELLOW JELLO

This theater game will mold players into a bowl of jiggling gelatin.

EQUIPMENT

None

SITUATION

Open area

TIME

10 minutes

DIRECTIONS

1. Gather players into a close group. Tell them that they have been changed into a bowl of banana Jello (or any flavor you like).

2. Pretend you are shaking the bowl. Begin slowly waving your hands as if you were conducting an orchestra. Jiggle quickly and vibrate the Jello more. Players are encouraged to act exactly the way Jello would.

3. Stop shaking the Jello. Usually Jello will shake for awhile until it slows down to a stop. Naturally, if you leave your Jello out in the sun, it will begin to melt away all over the ground.

VARIATION

Jumpin' Jello is a flavorful follow-the-leader variation. Divide the group into two "bowls" of Jello, say peach and raspberry. Two leaders are selected to shake up each bowl. The two groups of flavors stand mixed together in one group. Leaders stand in front of the groups and begin jiggling their flavors simultaneously as players follow their respective leader. In this game, leaders can make their Jello hop on one foot, twist, turn, shimmy, or shake a leg.

COPY CAT

In this whodunit, no one knows who is copying who.

EQUIPMENT

None

SITUATION

Open area

TIME

10 minutes

DIRECTIONS

1. Players stand in a circle.

2. Without letting anyone else know, every player secretly picks a person to watch. A player copies the movements of the watched player, exaggerating them very slightly. If no one seems to be moving, have players spin around once. While the group is still moving a bit, players should begin to mimic.

3. The movements of the group will eventually become larger and larger and usually everyone will end up doing the same thing without ever knowing who started it.

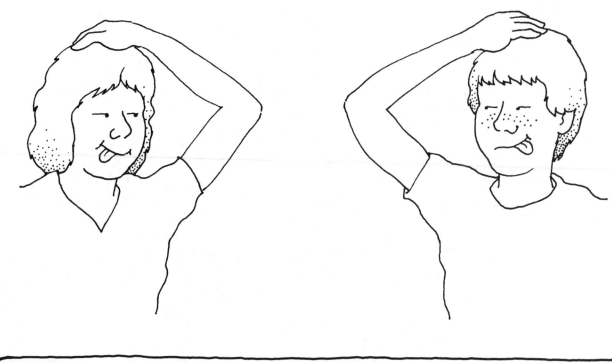

SAYS WHO?

Simon never said his game couldn't be changed.
So here's a game in which Simon says that
players are not eliminated.

MATERIALS

None

SITUATION

Open area

TIME

15 minutes

DIRECTIONS

1. Divide the group into two groups.
2. Choose one player to be Simon and to stand in front of the two groups of players. Any player being caught by Simon isn't out of the game; instead, that player switches groups.
3. Simon performs gestures and says, "Simon says do this." Whatever Simon says to do, players must do. Simon is a tricky person, however, and every now and then will simply say "Do this!" without saying "Simon says." In this instance, if a player gets confused and moves, he or she must change groups.
4. The game continues with groups changing players. The ideal end happens when one entire group loses and joins the other group to become winners.

VARIATION

1. The group is divided into two teams.
2. Each team selects a player to be Simon.
3. Each Simon tries to catch as many players as possible on their team who move without permission. Players who are caught switch over to the other team.
4. The smallest team after three minutes is the winner.

TICK-TACK-TOO

Here's an example of how a small game can have a big effect. The rules are the same as in the small version, but the change in scale provides some new "cross-examinations."

EQUIPMENT

Several pieces of chalk

SITUATION

Open pavement

TIME

25 minutes

DIRECTIONS

  1. Draw an expanded tick-tack-toe grid with 16 or 25 spaces on the pavement with squares the size of a hopscotch board. The players are divided into two teams—the 0 team and the X team.
  2. The rules are the same as traditional tick-tack-toe. The first team to complete a line horizontally, vertically, or diagonally across the playing field using team members scores a point.
  3. After both teams have agreed on which team will go first, the first team collects in a huddle to decide in which square a team member should stand. The players standing in the squares hold their arms over their heads in an X or an 0 to indicate the team.
  4. Teams alternate turns until one team has won. Players standing in the grid go back to their respective teams, and two new players start another round.

LAUGHING MATTER

This game explores the old saying, "He who laughs last, laughs best."

EQUIPMENT

None

SITUATION

Dry grassy area

TIME

5 minutes

DIRECTIONS

1. A dry grassy area is needed for this game. A single person is selected to be the Laugh Igniter. He or she lies down on the grass.

2. The rest of the group is divided into two groups. A player from each group lies down on either side of the Laugh Igniter with his or her head on the Laugh Igniter's stomach.

3. One by one players lie down placing their heads on the stomach of the last player. This makes two branches of players with the Laugh Igniter at the center connecting them both. This is useful when shy boys and girls prefer separate groups.

4. After everyone is arranged, the Laugh Igniter takes a deep breath and yells "Ha!" The two people resting on his or her stomach yell "Ha ha!" The people resting on their stomachs yell "Ha ha ha!" and so forth. The idea, of course, is that each person adds to the number of "ha's" at each turn.

5. Suggest that players yell in different tones of voice and rhythms. Some "Ho ho's" or "hee hee's" wouldn't hurt either. If the group hasn't been reduced to total hysteria, reverse the sequence and start from the end of the branches, reducing the number of "ha's."

ELEPHANT, PALM TREE, CAMEL

People have gone mad in the scorching heat of the desert. Some begin to imagine they see elephants, palm trees, and camels. Players in this game try to represent the mirages in order to humor the madness of the person who is It.

EQUIPMENT

None

SITUATION

Open area

TIME

10 minutes

DIRECTIONS

   1. One person is selected to be It. The rest of the group stands in a circle with the person who is It in the center.

   2. Before players begin, they must learn the three-person combinations that form the Elephant, Palm Tree, or Camel.

- Elephant: One person stands with arms pointed straight out in front like an elephant trunk. The two players on either side cup their hands behind the ears of the center person to make the elephant's ears.
- Palm Tree: All three players stand together as one trunk with arms raised in the air to imitate the swaying palms.
- Camel: The person in the center bends over while the players on either side supply humps with their fists.

All three players must act simultaneously to make one form.

   3. To play, the person who is It spins around trying to catch the players standing in the circle off-guard. When he or she points to a player and says "Camel!" (or "Elephant!" or "Palm Tree!"), the person selected becomes the center of the formation while the others on either side snap into shape. The person who is It counts to three. If one of the three people hesitates a fraction too long and doesn't complete the form or makes the wrong formation, he or she becomes the next It and changes places with the person in the center.

   4. After everyone feels laughed out, try one last rapid-fire round. Without switching the person who is It, players who make mistakes are eliminated until the three fastest formations are left.

DANGLING DONUT EATING CONTEST

Pie eating contests are hilarious—especially when faces are turned into blueberry blobs. Unfortunately, blueberry pies are expensive and no matter how big the sweet tooth, most kids can't eat a whole pie. This variation is just as much fun and is kinder to pocketbooks and stomachs.

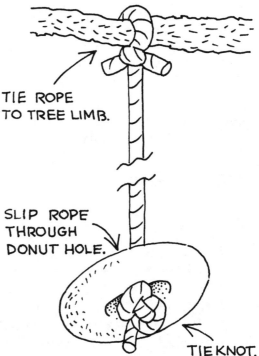

TIE ROPE TO TREE LIMB.

SLIP ROPE THROUGH DONUT HOLE.

TIE KNOT.

EQUIPMENT
A donut and a piece of clothesline rope for each player

SITUATION
A tree or jungle gym on a playground

TIME
20 minutes

DIRECTIONS
  1. Buy a donut for each contestant. Powdered sugar donuts are fun because players get white noses.
  2. Tie a rope, one for each player, to the branches of a tree or jungle gym. Keep ropes long enough so that they are only 2 or 3 feet off the ground. Slip the other end of the rope through the donut hole and knot it so that the donut doesn't slip off.
  3. The object of the game is to be the first player to eat an entire donut without using any hands.
  4. Players stand next to their donuts with their hands behind their backs. When the leader says "Go," players begin to gobble.
  5. The first player to completely consume a donut raises his or her arms in the air and yells "Whole in one!" before receiving the coveted "Crazy Cruller" award.

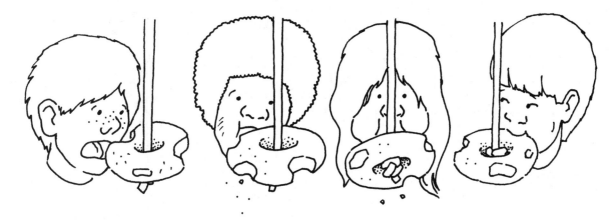

TUBE TEST

Nimble feet and a cool head are in order for this tiptoe through the tubes.

EQUIPMENT

6 carpet tubes
Hand saw

SITUATION

Small flat area

TIME

20 minutes

CUT TUBES INTO SMALLER SECTIONS.

DIRECTIONS

1. Collect six carpet tubes (a carpet store will be happy to save them) and cut them in half with a hand saw. You should then have a dozen tubes about two or three feet long.

2. Arrange the tubes in a row about a foot apart from each other.

3. Everyone lines up to take a turn walking through the obstacle course. Players must take one step in each space and are out if a tube is touched or moved.

4. After each player has taken a turn, the leader is allowed to move the front tube to the rear, placing it very close or outrageously far from the neighboring tube.

5. The last person to prance successfully through the course without moving a tube is "tubey" the winner.

TIGHTROPE WALKING

Unlike the brave high-wire walkers in the circus, players won't have far to fall with their tightropes on the ground. But like the skilled circus performers, they will have to keep their balance.

EQUIPMENT
20 yards of clothesline rope

SITUATION
Open playground

TIME
15 minutes

DIRECTIONS
1. Stretch two parallel ropes across the playground, keeping them on the ground, three or four feet apart. Tie the ends to trees, fences, or playground equipment.

2. To walk the "tightrope," place the heel of one foot on the start line and begin to walk—placing the heel of one foot directly to the toe of the other foot—all the way to the finish line.

3. Divide the group into two teams. When the leader says "Go," members of each team begin on their tightropes. Each player waits until the person ahead is finished "walking the rope" before beginning. The first team to finish walking the tightrope is the winner.

VARIATION
Create a rope obstacle course by laying out the rope in a squiggly line or in curves and loops.

HOPALONG

Dance instructor Arthur Murray would create elaborate footprint charts to show students the right way to rhumba or tango. In this activity, players won't learn the fox trot, but they will certainly be in step.

EQUIPMENT

Several pieces of chalk for each player

SITUATION

Open paved area or sidewalk

TIME

25 minutes

DIRECTIONS

1. Give each player a piece of chalk.
2. Instruct players to create a footprint course in which players can hop from print to print. Players trace around their shoes, spacing prints close together for quick hops, apart for long jumps, single prints for one-foot hops, and a mixture of routes that send hoppers around corners and spinning into spirals.
3. After players finish connecting footprints into one big game board, everyone lines up ready to hop aboard. The object of the game is to develop coordination, agility, balance, and to have lots of fun.

VARIATIONS

Have the lead hopper add follow-the-leader gestures. Have hoppers jump in clapping rhythm or hop in time to the beat of recorded music. Play a short, fast piece so that players really have to hop to it to finish or a long, slow piece so that hopping players become graceful ballet dancers.

LINE SWITCH

Both teams must work together to accomplish this cooperative switch-a-roo.

EQUIPMENT

Chalk

SITUATION

Paved area

TIME

15 minutes

DIRECTIONS

1. Divide the group into two teams.

2. On a sidewalk or paved area, draw a line of squares with a piece of chalk. Allow one space for each player. Leave an empty square in the center between the two groups. The object of the game is for all the players on one side of the blank space to switch places with the players on the other side.

3. Have players stand in the squares. One team will be on one side of the empty square, one team on the other. To begin, the leader yells "Line Switch!"

4. One at a time, players may move forward into the free spot or jump over an occupied space to a free one. Only one player is allowed per space.

5. When both teams have successfully maneuvered to the opposite side of the empty center square, everyone wins.

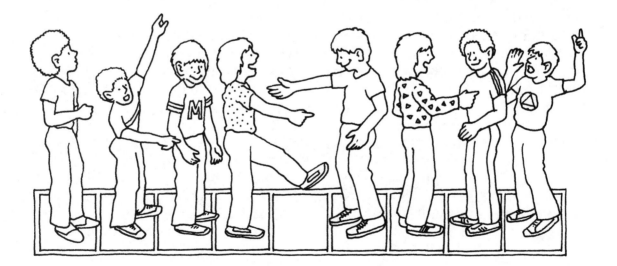

SIDEWALK MURALS

It took Michelangelo four years to transform the ceiling of the Sistine Chapel into a masterpiece, but it will take players only moments to change the sidewalk into the world's largest drawing.

EQUIPMENT

Several dozen pieces of chalk in various colors

SITUATION

A sidewalk or paved area

TIME

30 minutes

DIRECTIONS

1. Gather players together and discuss ideas for a group drawing. You might begin by saying, "We're going to make the world's largest drawing," and ask players if they have any suggestions for a theme. A single design with lots of decorative parts, such as a butterfly or a fiery dragon, provides an overall structure that can be filled in any way players wish.

2. To begin, draw a simple outline of the shape. For example, if players agree on drawing a snake, you should draw two parallel serpentine lines down the entire sidewalk.

3. Give players several pieces of colored chalk and have them fill in the outline with patterns and shapes—stars, dots, squiggles, checks, and so forth. The finished drawing will be a patchwork of all the players' designs combined into one large picture.

VARIATIONS

1. Have players trace each other's shadows. Have them turn, stretch, crouch, and so forth to change the shape of their shadows.

2. Suggest to players that they trace the same shadow shape several times to create a pattern or overlap shapes to make new shapes inside.

3. Players can fill shapes in with colors and textures to make a giant unified picture.

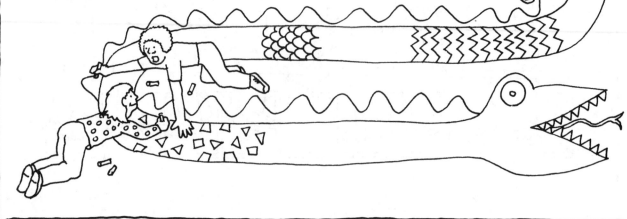

FENCE WEAVING

Fences are enclosures or barriers that keep you in or out. The goal of this activity is to transform a plain fence into a decorative weaving, to warm up unfriendly barricades, and to make them "de-fence-less."

EQUIPMENT

Fabric scraps, ribbons, felt pieces
Yarn
String
Sticks, twigs, and leaves
Scissors

SITUATION

A wire or slatted fence

TIME

35 minutes

DIRECTIONS

1. Collect a large amount of fabric scraps, ribbons, and yarn as well as leaves, twigs, and long reeds. Use scissors to cut fabric and yarn into shapes and lengths you will use.
2. Before players begin, explore some design ideas. Players may want to weave lines of yarn and sticks that intersect, curve, and zigzag across the entire length of the fence. Lines might be narrow or turn into broad shapes. Certain areas of the fence might be woven of twigs while another part might be covered with thin, knotted fabric scraps.
3. Players begin to weave materials in and out of wires and slats. Encourage individual players to make their designs a part of the entire group weaving.
4. Finished weavings are not only nice to look at, but they also make wonderful backdrops for other playful activities.

GOOD IMPRESSIONS

A rubbing is a picture made by holding a piece of paper over a raised or textured surface and rubbing it with a crayon. The result is a picture of the object.

EQUIPMENT

A piece of paper for each player (Have a few
   extra pieces on hand for those who make
   mistakes or who are very prolific.)
A crayon for each player

SITUATION

A relief or textured surface

TIME

30 minutes

DIRECTIONS

1. Give each player a piece of paper and a crayon.
2. With players, search around the area for things to rub such as metal plaques on buildings, cornerstones, architectural decorations, sewer covers, tombstones (a traditional favorite), or leaves on the sidewalk. Anything flat with a texture will work.
3. When everyone has found a surface to rub, first brush off the rubbing surface. Next, peel the wrapper off the crayon and hold the paper firmly over the object. Rub the side of the crayon over the surface. Don't bear down too hard—rubbings will look nicer.
4. After players have completed their rubbings, collect them. Show each one to the group. Have players give their impressions of each, guessing where each rubbing came from and the places that seem best to rub.

PEEK THROUGH

If you've ever been to an old-time carnival, you may remember those funny painted screens with holes cut out where people's heads should be. When people placed their heads in the holes it looked like they were flying in a biplane or walking on a tightrope. This project is bound to have an effect on the players' self-images.

DOOR

HOLE
FOR FACE

EQUIPMENT

Appliance shipping box for a refrigerator
Utility knife
Pencil for each player
Tempera paint in various colors
Cups for the paint
Brushes for each cup

SITUATION

Open area

TIME

45 minutes

DIRECTIONS

1. Have players decide on scenes to paint on the sides of the appliance box. Some traditional ideas are a juggling clown, a weight-lifting muscle man, a baby in a carriage, and a banana-eating monkey. But players may want to use outer space, sports, TV, or fantasy creatures as an inspiration.

3. Cut a door opening on one side of the box. On the other three sides, players draw their scenes. Draw an oval shape wherever a face is to appear (measure a child's head to get the proper proportions).

4. Cut out face holes with a utility knife.

5. Players fill in the drawings with paint.

6. Use Peek Throughs to create instant tableaus or to provide unique settings for photos. Place a mirror in front so that peeking players can see their new images.

SLOTTED SHAPES

You may have built a house with slotted rectangular cards. They are fun, but the results are somewhat predictable. What if the cards came in odd shapes and sizes? Any predictions?

EQUIPMENT

Sheets of corrugated cardboard for each player
  (Sheets can be cut from appliance or furniture boxes. Ask store owners to save them for you.)
Hand-held jigsaw with a fine blade
A long, heavy-duty extension cord
Several utility knives
Tempera paint in assorted colors
Cups for paint
Brushes for each cup
Pencil for each player

SITUATION

Flat open area

TIME

45 minutes (allow for preparation time before the actual event)

DIRECTIONS

1. Organize materials in several different areas—a cutting area, a drawing and painting area, and a drying area.
2. Give each player a piece of cardboard on which to draw a shape. Shapes should be kept simple but playful—a wavy scallop, a curvy crescent, a starburst, a triangle, an amoeba, or any other whimsical single shape.

1. DRAW SHAPE.

2. CUT OUT.

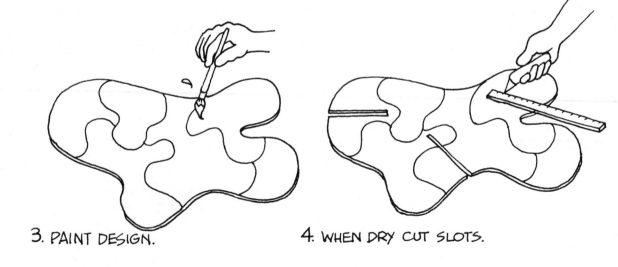

3. PAINT DESIGN.

4. WHEN DRY CUT SLOTS.

3. As players finish drawing shapes, they line up in the cutting area. A teacher or one or two responsible players who have been taught how to safely use utility knives and a jigsaw should cut the shapes. Curves can be cut easily with a jigsaw while the knives work best with straight lines.

4. Once shapes are cut, players begin decorating with tempera paints and brushes. Suggest to players that designs be kept simple—stripes, dots, checks, and patterns of all kinds. Warn players not to mix brushes and paints, because colors will get muddy.

5. While one side of the shapes are drying, have players designate where and how many slots are to be cut. Five to eight slots usually work well. Cut slots with utility knife when shapes are dry. Flip shapes over and paint the other side.

6. When shapes are dry, players combine their shapes, carefully slipping them together one by one, to form a sculpture. The finished structure will be as surprising as the shapes that make it.

SPACE RACE

This space race takes place in the outer spaces of the playground.

EQUIPMENT

Roll of fishing or nylon line
Sausage-shaped balloon for each player
Drinking straw for each player
9" x 12" sheet of construction paper for each
   player
Stapler to share
An assortment of felt markers to share
Roll of masking tape

SITUATION

Open area

TIME

35 minutes

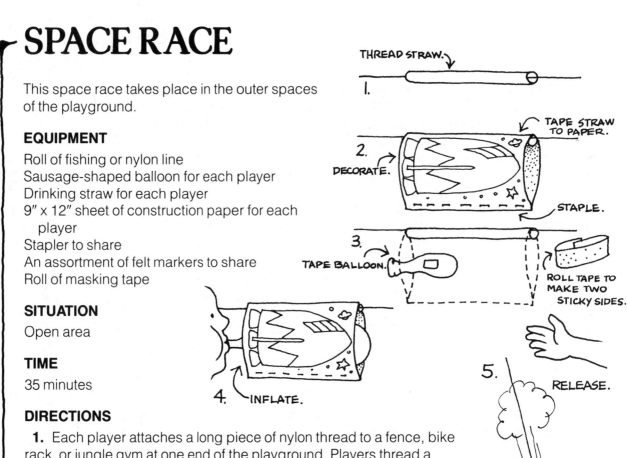

DIRECTIONS

   1. Each player attaches a long piece of nylon thread to a fence, bike rack, or jungle gym at one end of the playground. Players thread a drinking straw onto their piece of nylon and attach the other end on the opposite side of the playground, pulling and stretching the string as tightly as possible.

   2. Give each player a piece of 9- by 12-inch construction paper. Players fold the construction paper in half and decorate it with space graphics using felt markers to create their own UFO.

   3. Everyone hangs the paper over the straw and tapes it in place. The paper is stapled together on the bottom, leaving the front and back open.

   4. Players attach a deflated balloon to the inside of the paper with a piece of masking tape. The opening of the balloon should stick out the back of the construction paper pocket.

   5. Players line up with their rockets and blow up their balloons, pinching the ends until the leader gives the launch signal.

   6. All players join the leader in a countdown. On the word "Blast off!" players release their rockets. The escaping air propels rockets forward. The rocket to make it the farthest—or the first rocket to make it across the playground galaxy—is the winner.

TIRE DECORATION

A pile of old tires isn't very appealing to look at but scrounge around for free old tires at service stations and tire companies. (You'll need a truck and some volunteers to search the area and collect the tires.) This decorative project will add pizzazz to rejected treads and change the complexion of any playground.

EQUIPMENT

30 to 40 old tires
Approximately 4 gallons of water-based outdoor trim paint in bright colors
12 to 18 paint cups or buckets
A paint brush for each cup
A bucket of water for clean-up

SITUATION

A grassy area or yard that wouldn't be damaged by paint

TIME

Two days or play sessions

DIRECTIONS

1. Divide the group into smaller groups of three people. Give each group three or four cups of paint, each cup having its own brush. Divide the tires among the groups.

2. Before players begin to decorate, discuss ideas with the group. Have them suggest designs—spirals, stripes, flowers, and so forth.

3. Players paint as much of the tire as possible without moving it. To avoid muddying the colors, make sure that players don't mix colors and brushes. After players have finished one side of the tires, allow them to dry overnight before turning them over to paint the other side.

4. The next day, finish painting the other side of the tires. Allow them to thoroughly dry before rolling them off the "assembly" line into the eager hands of players. Tires can be stacked into towers, forts, and castles and can be used as props for games (see Tireless Tires, pages 82–83).

TIRELESS TIRES

After tires have been painted and transformed into colorful works of art, they're ready to be used for the art of play. Here are a few variations.

EQUIPMENT

30 to 40 tires
50' of clothesline rope
A box of chalk

SITUATION

Paved area or open yard

TIME

15 minutes each

DIRECTIONS

Note: Tires can be heavy for small children. Divide groups of children into pairs for tire throwing.

Far Flung

Gather players in a line. Give each player a turn to toss a tire. The player who throws a tire the farthest is the winner.

Higher Tire

Tie a rope across the play area about three feet above the ground. Give each player a turn to toss a tire over the rope. After each player has had a turn, raise the rope a bit higher. Those who were able to get their tire over the rope line up for a second round. Continue raising the rope after each round. The last player left is the winner.

Tire Ring

Create a tossing course with rocks, stumps, and poles in the ground. Divide players into two teams. Give each team a turn at throwing their tires to ring the targets. The team with the most ringers is the winner.

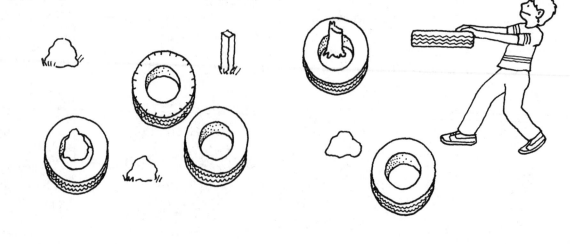

Roll Playing

Each player lines up with a tire at one end of an open paved area. When the leader says "Go," everyone gives his or her tire a push. The player whose tire rolls the farthest is the winner.

Roll Race

Players line up with their tires at one end of a paved area. Mark a finish line at the other end. When the leader says "Go," players give their tires a push. The first tire over the finish line is the winner.

Tire Pinball

With a piece of chalk, draw a large gameboard grid on an open paved area. Fill in the squares with scores and instructions such as "miss a turn," "roll again," "double your last score," or "minus 3 points." Players roll their tires onto the gameboard and try to make their tire land on a square. Players can either have a set amount of rolls or, if there are a lot of tires and just a few players, players can take turns rolling the tires on the board until it is filled with tires. The player with the most points is the winner.

Stack Up

Gather tires into one pile in the middle of the play area. Divide the group into two teams. When the leader says "Go," both teams race toward the pile of tires. Teams stack tires into a tower. The team who can build the highest tower in 30 seconds is the winner.

Of Course

Arrange tires in a double row as part of a larger obstacle course. When running players get to the tires, they must step in each one, alternately placing left feet in the left tires and right feet in the right tires. Players then race off to the next hurdle.

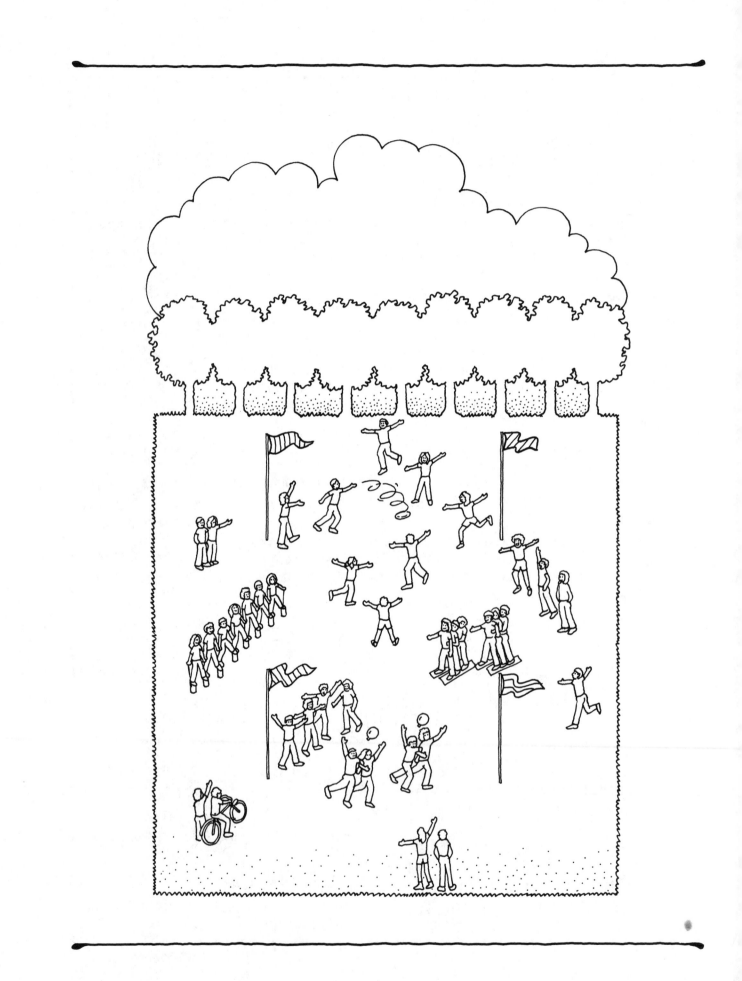

WIDE OPEN SPACES

Some active games need unobstructed space so that players can run, jump, hop, roll, and twist with safe enthusiasm.

LEMONADE

Lemon juice and sugar aren't necessary ingredients to play Lemonade. This charade game proves not to be a lemon as players squeeze their way back to their safety zones.

EQUIPMENT

None

SITUATION

Large open area

TIME

15 minutes

Speech bubble: YOU'RE AN EARTHQUAKE INVESTIGATOR FROM SAN FRANCISCO!

DIRECTIONS

1. Mark two goal lines about 10 or 15 yards apart. Divide players into two teams. Teams stand behind their goal lines and face each other.

2. One team is selected to go first. Huddling together, the first team chooses a country or city to represent and a trade or occupation particular to that country to be acted out. For example, players may be pearl divers from Japan or ice-fishing Eskimos from Alaska.

3. Both teams line up on their goal lines across from each other. The first team takes a giant step and shouts in an aggressive voice, "Here we come!" The second team responds in an equally assertive manner by taking a bigger step and shouting, "Where from?" The first team, getting a bit riled, takes another step and answers, "Italy!" (or wherever). The second team takes another step and asks, "What's your trade?" At which time the first team answers, "Lemonade!" By this time, both teams will be nose to nose. The second team then demands, "Show us some if you're not afraid!"

4. The first team acts out in pantomime a trade or occupation. For example, if they say they are from Italy they may act out pizza makers spinning dough in the air.

5. The second team tries to guess the charade. When someone identifies it correctly, the first team dashes back to the safety of their goal line; the second team gives chase and tries to tag them.

6. Tagged players join the second team. Teams switch roles and the second team chooses a place and an occupation. The game continues through an agreed number of turns, and the team with the most players is the winner.

OCTOPUS

Since this game needs an octopus and an ocean,
a little pretending is in order.

EQUIPMENT

None

SITUATION

Large open area

TIME

15 minutes

DIRECTIONS

1. Define two lines on either end of the playground about 15 or 20 yards apart. The lines are the "shores" and the "ocean" is the area in between.

2. One person is selected to be the Octopus. The Octopus wanders around the ocean while the rest of the players are swimmers standing on the shore behind one of the goal lines. The object of the game is for the swimmers to cross to the other shore without getting caught by the Octopus.

3. When the Octopus calls "Octopus!" swimmers dash across the waters. Those tagged by the Octopus freeze in place.

4. On the next round, those frozen become the tentacles of the Octopus, capable of tagging swimmers. Anyone caught is frozen and becomes another tentacle of the growing creature.

5. Inevitably, one lone player is left to take one last plunge before becoming the next Octopus.

HE REALLY GETS INTO THIS GAME.

ROCK, PAPER, SCISSORS

Certain traditional games cannot be omitted from sure-fire fun, and this game may top the list. Rock, Paper, Scissors has the benefit of years of play to ensure its place in game history.

EQUIPMENT

None

SITUATION

Large open area

TIME

15 minutes

DIRECTIONS

1. Divide the group into two teams. Designate a free zone at each end of the playground.

2. Gather the two teams in the center of the field and explain the rules. Players must remember three symbols—a fist is Rock, a flat hand is Paper, two fingers (held open to resemble the blades) are Scissors. Depending on the combination, one will be the winner. Paper covers Rock, Rock breaks Scissors, and Scissors cut Paper. For example, if one team has Rock and the other has Paper, Paper wins.

3. Each team forms a huddle in its free zone and agrees upon a symbol. This is chancy because nobody knows what the other team will pick. Teams meet back in the center with symbols in mind.

4. Both teams chant together, "Rock, Paper, Scissors . . ." and then all players of each team show their symbol. In a split second, teams decide who's the winner and who's the loser. Losers run back to their free zone with the winners in pursuit. Those tagged by the winners become members of their team. If both teams show the same symbol, teams rehuddle and play again.

5. Players play for a predetermined number of rounds. The team with the most players is the winner.

OVERALL UNDERSTANDING

In the heat of this game, players will have not only ups and downs, but also overs and outs.

EQUIPMENT

2 large balls (basketballs, beach balls, or balloons)

SITUATION

Open area

TIME

10 minutes

DIRECTIONS

1. Players are divided into two teams. Teams line up in parallel rows with players standing behind one another.

2. The first player on each team is given a basketball, beach ball, or balloon. When the leader says "Go," the first player on each line passes the ball backward over his or her head to the second player. The second player passes the ball under his or her legs to the next person behind, and so forth. The ball continues to be passed backward down the line, alternately over and under, until it reaches the last player.

3. The last player, receiving the ball, runs to the front of his or her line and begins to pass the ball backward again.

4. This continues until every player on the line has a chance to be at the beginning. The team whose first player gets to the front of the line again first is the winner.

VARIATION

1. On one end of the playground, form a single line with the entire group. Four or five balls or balloons will be needed to play.

2. One by one, the first person takes each ball or balloon and passes it backward overhead to the next person. The next player passes it under his or her legs to the next player, and this continues alternately down the line.

3. When the last player receives a ball, he or she runs to the front of the line and starts again. With four or five balls moving down the line, and players running to the front of the line, the line will move slowly across the playground.

PASSED OVER

Players will not be able to pass up this fast-paced game.

EQUIPMENT

Ball

SITUATION

Open area

TIME

10 minutes

DIRECTIONS

1. Players form two lines about four feet apart and face each other.

2. The player at the start of one line tosses a ball across to the player at the start of the other line.

3. After the player tosses the ball, he or she runs to the end of the other line.

4. The player catches the ball, throws it to the next player on the other line, and then runs to the end of the opposite line.

5. This continues until the players on both lines are reversed. The game may continue with both lines taking a giant step backward to increase the space between them.

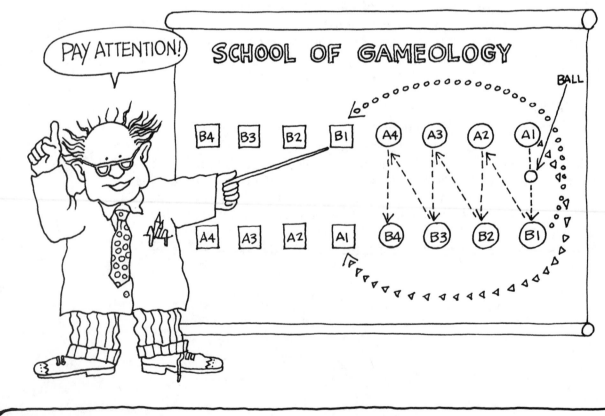

HOG CALL

Although Pig Latin is not required, a good set of lungs is suggested for this down-home game of match making.

EQUIPMENT
None

SITUATION
Open area

TIME
10 minutes

DIRECTIONS

1. Divide the group into pairs.
2. Each pair decides on a pair of things to be. For example:

- Hearts and flowers
- Beans and franks
- Bow and arrow
- Cloak and dagger
- Skin and bones
- Milk and honey
- Tar and feather
- Nuts and bolts
- Sweet and sour

One partner picks one of the pair of things while the other partner picks the other one.

3. Players scatter around the playground. All players close their eyes and start shouting the name of whatever object their partner picked. The point of the game is to reunite the partners. It's difficult to distinguish one call from another while everyone is shouting. Occasionally, two pairs will select the same things to shout, which results in some mismatched matches.

4. The game ends when all pairs have been matched and the last players open their eyes.

ECHO

If you stood at the edge of the Grand Canyon and yelled "Hello!" your voice would bounce back and forth between the canyon walls, repeating the sound over and over and causing an echo. In this game the players are like the Grand Canyon, and their whispers bounce from person to person.

EQUIPMENT

None

SITUATION

Large open area

TIME

10 minutes

DIRECTIONS

1. Designate start and finish points, such as a wall or a tree, at either end of the playground. Divide players into two teams. Teams stand in two lines on opposite sides of the playground.

2. Facing each other, both teams count off by twos. The "twos" from one team then change places with the "twos" from the other team. Each player should now be facing a member of the opposite team as well as having a member of the opposing team on either side.

3. The leader gathers the first player from each team at the start point and whispers a short sentence to each one.

4. Upon hearing the sentence, both players run to the second players on their teams and repeat the whisper as clearly as possible. The second players run to the opposite line and whisper to the third players. Players continue to zigzag back and forth across the playground, passing the sentence from player to player.

5. The last player from each team to hear the sentence runs to the finish point and shouts out the sentence. If the first player to reach the finish point shouts the correct sentence, his or her team is the winner. If the second player to reach it shouts the correct sentence and the first player was wrong, then the second team is the winner. If neither player shouts the correct original sentence, the leader decides which of the two sentences shouted is closer to the original.

VARIATION

1. Divide players into two teams. Each team forms a line with players standing as far apart as possible. Teams might extend down the street, across a field, or around a building.

2. Each team is given a word—something silly such as "banana split," "flapjack," "snafu," or "guru."

3. The leader stands in the middle between the two lines and shouts "Go" to begin the echo. The echo is started at one end of one team and at the opposite end of the other team and is shouted from team member to team member. The word can be called out only after the previous player shouts it.

4. It is easy for players to jump ahead and shout the echo before it is passed on to them. To help avoid this, have players run and tag the next player before shouting the word.

5. The last player in a team to shout the word runs to tag the leader. The first team to complete their echo is the winner.

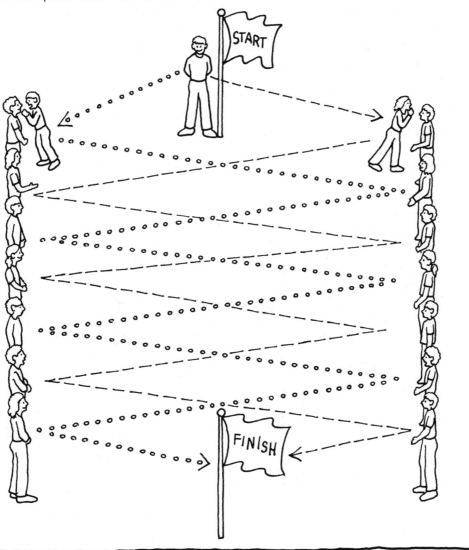

ESCORT

Introductions, bowing, and other social formalities may be compromised a bit in this game. The proper decorum is simply unabashed enthusiasm.

EQUIPMENT

None

SITUATION

Open area

TIME

10 minutes

DIRECTIONS

1. Divide the group into two or more teams of six or more players.
2. Mark start and finish lines about 15 yards apart. The object is for each team to get all its players from the start line to the finish line.
3. Teams line up behind the start line. At a signal from the leader, the first player on each team takes the hand of the second player and runs across the playground to the finish line.
4. The first player remains at the finish line while the second player runs back to his or her team to escort the third player. The second player stays at the finish line while the third player goes back for the fourth player and so on.
5. This continues until one team wins by getting its entire team across the finish line.

FOOT LOOSE

The only way to rid the planet Instep of its arch enemy—the Flatfoot Plague—is for players to carry each sole to the safety of the planet Podiatry.

EQUIPMENT
None

SITUATION
Open area

TIME
10 minutes

DIRECTIONS

1. The object of this game is to transport everyone from one end of the playground to the other. To heighten the challenge and make the game more fun, suggest that players are fleeing a dreaded disease and can only escape if they are carried by other players.

2. Players may be carried by as many players as necessary. When the carried player is delivered to the other side of the playground, the others must go back and carry each other. This continues until the last player is carried by a single person.

3. The last player, who was not carried, gets carried back triumphantly to the rescued planet on the shoulders of the entire group.

JEEPERS CREEPERS

Players are prone to get the creeps as they creep through the grass in a prone position.

EQUIPMENT

A roll of crepe paper for each team

SITUATION

Open grassy area

TIME

15 minutes

DIRECTIONS

1. Divide the group into teams of three. Each team receives a roll of crepe paper.

2. Mark two parallel boundary lines about 10 yards apart. Each team lines up behind one of the boundaries.

3. When the leader says "Go," two players on each team get down on their hands and knees, one behind the other. The rear player places his or her hands on the ankles of the front player. The third team member becomes the connector and connects the other two players by wrapping the wrist and ankle pairs together with the crepe paper.

4. After players have been connected, they begin to creep toward the opposite boundary. If the crepe paper tears, the two crawlers must stop while the third player repairs the connection.

5. Once the two crawlers reach the opposite boundary, they unwrap themselves, and one switches places with the third player. The next connector wraps up the crawlers, and they creep back across to the other side.

6. When the crawlers have reached the original boundary, the players switch again so that each team member has wrapped the other two. The first team to cross the boundary line after all three team members have been crawlers and connectors is the winner.

WRAP CREPE PAPER.

CENTIPEDE

No matter how you slice it, this game proves that
the whole is greater than the sum of its parts.

EQUIPMENT

None

SITUATION

Open grassy area

TIME

10 minutes

DIRECTIONS

1. Divide players into two teams.
2. Mark start and finish lines about 30 feet apart.
3. Teams line up with one person behind the other, facing the finish line. Next, players sit down and wrap their legs around the person in front to form the body of the centipede. Players' arms become the legs.
4. When the leader says "Go," players lift with their arms and begin to push the centipede toward the finish line. If players become separated, they must try and reconnect.
5. The winning centipede must completely cross the finish line with all its players connected.

ROW RACE

Players propel themselves by the seat of their pants without benefit of water or an oar as they sail across the playground.

EQUIPMENT

None

SITUATION

Open grassy area

TIME

10 minutes

DIRECTIONS

1. The group is divided into pairs. Mark a short course with the start and finish lines about 15 or 20 feet apart.

2. Pairs line up. Partner A sits on the starting line with knees together and legs extended straight out. Partner B sits facing Partner A with soles of shoes together, knees bent, and hands clasped. To move, Partner B pulls Partner A into a bent-knee position. Partner B then pushes back to straighten his or her legs. Next, Partner A straightens his or her legs and pushes Partner B's legs into a bent position. This pushing and pulling motion resembles rowing and moves players along at about a yard at a time.

3. The first pair to completely row across the finish line is the winner.

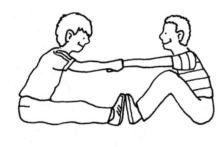

1.

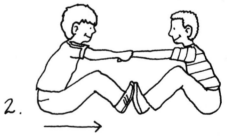

2.

3.

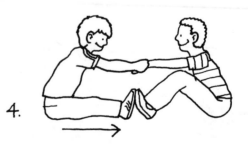

4.

RACING FORMS

Here's a human race with physical traits not found in any anthropological study.

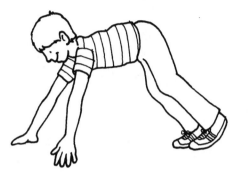

EQUIPMENT

None

SITUATION

Open grassy area

TIME

10 minutes

DIRECTIONS

1. Mark start and finish lines about 30 or 40 feet apart.
2. Players line up at the start line. Just before the leader says "Go," he or she shouts out the form in which players must race:

- Spider: Players bend over and walk on their hands and feet, not on their knees.
- Backward Spider: Players walk backward on their hands and feet, stomachs up, keeping their bodies off the ground.
- Crab: Players sit down with their knees drawn up in front of them, lift their bodies off the ground, and walk on their hands and feet in a sitting position.
- Roll: Players lie down on their side and roll to the finish line.
- Flamingo: Players hop on one foot.

Players may want to invent other forms before the race.

3. The first player to the finish line with the proper form is the winner.

VARIATION

Divide the race course into three or four segments. The leader determines which form must be used to travel through each segment. Players change form as they move through each segment, or the leader can call out names of different forms as players race across the play field. Players change form accordingly.

HULK

At the mere mention of the name, quiet groups of people begin the terrible transformation into the horrible Hulk!

EQUIPMENT

None

SITUATION

Open area

TIME

10 minutes

DIRECTIONS

1. Divide players into two teams. Define start and finish lines about 10 or 15 yards apart.
2. Each team transforms into the hideous Hulk by interlocking arms, riding piggyback, holding hands, or by any other creative means.
3. The only rule is that the number of arms and legs that may be used for walking is determined by subtracting two from the number of people that make up each Hulk. For example, if there are ten people on a team, only eight legs and eight arms may be used for moving.
4. Both Hulks assemble on the start line. When the leader says "Go," both monsters creep toward the finish line. The first Hulk to completely cross over the line is the winner.

BOARD SHUFFLE

Unlike the game of Shuffleboard, players really shuffle along on cardboard.

EQUIPMENT

4 pieces of 36″ x 6″ corrugated cardboard
12 strips of fabric, approximately 20″ x 5″
Scissors

SITUATION

Open grassy area

TIME

15 minutes

DIRECTIONS

1. Select six players. Divide them equally into two teams. Mark start and finish lines about 20 feet apart.

2. Team members, one behind the other, line up behind the start line. Each team straddles two pieces of cardboard like skis, placing their right feet on one piece of cardboard and their left feet on the other. The leader secures the feet to the cardboard by punching a hole with a scissors in the cardboard on either side of each foot. Run a cloth strip through the holes and under the cardboard, then tie it around each foot like a sandal.

3. Players stand ready at the start line while holding onto each other's waist. When the leader says "Go," teams begin to shuffle toward the finish line. Team members can coordinate steps by chanting "left, right, left, right . . ."

4. The first team to shuffle over the finish line is the winner.

WACKY WALKERS

If you've ever walked on the wild side, this game
will add a new twist. Players go through strange
gyrations as they move around a Frisbee axis.

EQUIPMENT

A Frisbee or a paper plate for each pair of players

SITUATION

Open area

TIME

15 minutes

DIRECTIONS

1. Divide the group into pairs. Give each pair a Frisbee or a paper plate.

2. Mark start and finish lines about 10 yards apart.

3. Pairs line up at the start line. Partners hold their plate or Frisbee
between them. The object of the game is to race to the finish line as fast as
possible while stepping over the Frisbee or paper plate, one foot at a time,
without letting go of it.

4. When the leader says "Go," partners twist and turn, each taking a turn
to step. Although this is not difficult to do, it can be confusing so players
should start off slowly. Players that let go of their Frisbee must go back to
the line and start again.

5. The first pair to cross the finish line is the winner.

HOOPLA

This is a hoop hop for hoopful players.

EQUIPMENT

A hula hoop for each player

SITUATION

Open space

TIME

10 minutes

DIRECTIONS

1. Mark start and finish lines about 30 or 40 feet apart. Players line up at the start line, each holding a hula hoop. If there are only a few hula hoops to share, divide players into smaller groups for several races.

2. When the leader says "Go," each player places his or her hoop on the ground in front at a reasonable jumping distance.

3. Players jump into their hoops, pull them up over their heads, and toss them again to move toward the finish line. Players who fail to make their jump into the hoop must go back to the start line and begin again.

4. The first player to hop over the finish line into his or her hoop gets a "Hoop, hoop, hooray!"

CLAWS

You've heard of people clawing their way to the top, here's an opportunity to see it in action.

EQUIPMENT
Paper towel tubes
Construction paper
Tape
Scissors
A balloon for each player (Round ones are best.)
Cardboard box or plastic bag

SITUATION
Open area

TIME
20 minutes

DIRECTIONS
1. You'll need to make 12 paper claws, 6 for each team. Claws can be paper towel tubes or may be made by rolling a piece of construction paper around a tube, taping it, and slipping it off.

2. Blow up one balloon for each player. The small round ones work best. Keep balloons in a big cardboard box or plastic bag so that they don't blow away.

3. Mark a boundary line and place the box of balloons about 20 or 30 feet away.

4. Each team lines up behind the boundary line. The first member of each team slips three claws on each hand. When the leader says "Go," players race toward the container of balloons. Players pick up a balloon with their claws and race back to their waiting teams.

5. If the wind snatches the balloon away, players may run and catch it. If the balloon pops or blows beyond the boundaries, players must return to their team with empty claws.

6. The next team member takes the claws and does the same. Players continue to race back and forth collecting balloons. The team who collects the most balloons is the winner, claws down.

BACKLASH

Stand back and get ready for a back-to-back relay race from backstretch to homestretch.

EQUIPMENT
4 round balloons (with extras just in case)

SITUATION
Large open area

TIME
10 minutes

DIRECTIONS

1. Divide the group into two teams, then divide each team into pairs. This is a relay race, and the racecourse can extend across a large field or around a building.

2. Mark the start and finish lines. On a circular track, players can begin and end at the same place.

3. Teams of pairs space themselves equally from one end of the racecourse to the other. Pairs stand back to back with arms linked at the elbow.

4. Blow up four round balloons and give two each to the first pair from each team. One balloon is held in each hand of each player. When the leader says "Go," the first two pairs make their way to the next pair of linked players. The first pair transfers its balloons to the next pair. Walking and transferring the balloons takes some coordination while arms are linked.

5. The relay of balloons continues from pair to pair. The first pair to cross the finish line wins with the backing of the whole team!

BALLOON DUO

This two-fisted balloon game will have twosomes
doing a two-step.

EQUIPMENT

A round balloon for each pair of players

SITUATION

Open area on a calm day

TIME

20 minutes

DIRECTIONS

1. Divide players into pairs. Give each pair a balloon to inflate and tie.
2. Mark start and finish lines about 30 or 40 feet apart. Partners stand side to side at the start line, linking their inside arms and holding the balloon in their free hands.
3. When the leader says "Go," partners work together hitting their balloon to keep it in the air and making their way across the playing field. If a balloon lands on the ground, partners may stop and pick it up but may not unlink arms.
4. The first pair of players to hit their balloon over the finish line gets a double dose of applause.

FOUR-WAY FRISBEE

This game features flinging Frisbees and fantastic finales in a fabulous frenzy of four-way fun.

EQUIPMENT

A Frisbee

SITUATION

Large open area

TIME

20 minutes

DIRECTIONS

1. Mark four goals at each corner of the playground. Divide the group into four teams, with a player from each team stationed at a goal.

2. The object of the game is for a team to get the Frisbee over its goal line to a team member. Gather teams into the center of the playing field. Toss the Frisbee randomly into the group.

3. Team members toss the Frisbee from player to player but are not allowed to run while carrying it. A player who intercepts a flying Frisbee cannot move before throwing it again. The other players are not allowed to interfere with players throwing the Frisbee.

4. Team members able to throw the Frisbee to the player at their goal win a point. The team members that win the most games out of a predetermined number are first-rate Frisbee flingers.

SPACE STATIONS

Pressurized space suits and antigravity boots are not required for this space trip, but some delicate maneuvering is needed as players go flying.

EQUIPMENT

3 to 5 Frisbees

SITUATION

Large open area

TIME

15 minutes

DIRECTIONS

 1. Three to five Frisbees are placed on the ground to become Space Stations. One person is selected to be Ground Control. The rest of the players are Astronauts floating through space, enjoying the lack of gravity and singing their favorite space theme.

 2. When Ground Control shouts "Red Alert!" the spaced-out players run to hook up with the nearest Space Station. Unfortunately, the last player to touch a Space Station is lost in space forever and is out of the game. This is tragic, but even more important is that *two* players cannot touch while hooking up to a Space Station or they are both out of the game.

 3. As Astronauts become better at locating Space Stations and the group gets smaller, Ground Control occasionally removes a Space Station until only one is left. The last person to survive a "Red Alert" is the next Ground Controller.

SMARTY CAT

Cats seem to have a mind of their own and will not be coerced into anything. Here a clever cat is given a workout with some deceptive humans.

EQUIPMENT

None

SITUATION

Large open area

TIME

10 minutes

DIRECTIONS

1. One player is selected to be the Cat while the rest of the group picks safety zones—trees, playground equipment, a bench, a flagpole, or spaces drawn with chalk—that are scattered around the area. The object of the game is for a player to switch safety zones with another player before the Cat steals it first.

2. The Cat stands in the center of the playground, which is determined by the location of the safety zones. Players try to distract the Cat by shouting "Here kitty, kitty," thereby providing a diversion so other players can switch.

3. When two players believe the Cat is not looking, they dash across the playing area to switch places. A smart Cat will pretend to look in the opposite direction while luring players behind to run. Unaware of the sneaky Cat's plans, a runner might not make it to a vacant zone before the Cat gets there first. However, once running begins, everyone usually joins in the confusion and abandons his or her safety zone for the thrill of danger.

4. The runner who gets caught without a safety zone is the next Smarty Cat.

TOUCH AND GO

This fast-paced game is particularly wild when everyone chooses the same thing to touch.

EQUIPMENT

None

SITUATION

Open area

TIME

10 minutes

DIRECTIONS

1. Divide the group into two teams. Both teams line up side by side in the middle of the playground facing the caller.

2. Teams arrange themselves in a specific order, such as by height, age, first letter of first name, and so forth.

3. The caller shouts the name of an object or thing found in the play area such as a tree or a fence. Players then break ranks, touch the object named, and reassemble rapidly in exactly the same order. Since this is a game of instant discovery, callers should add their own creative touches and name the things that are not usually noticed, for example:

- Touch a tiny twig
- Touch the knot in a tree
- Touch a crack in the sidewalk
- Touch the corner of the building
- Touch the hole in the fence

4. The team reassembling first most often after a predetermined number of calls is the winner—and should touch off a round of cheers.

VARIATION

Have callers call out the names of two, three, or four things.

LEG LEAP

It may seem like a roundabout way to see whose team is the fastest, but the excitement of players waiting for their turn to run will keep this game hopping.

EQUIPMENT

None

SITUATION

Flat grassy area

TIME

10 minutes

DIRECTIONS

1. Divide the group into two teams. An extra player can be the caller.
2. Teams sit facing each other. Players in each team extend their legs, keeping their knees together and having the soles of their feet touching to form pairs with players from the other team. Leave enough space between pairs of legs for players to hop over.
3. Pairs count off down the line. When the caller shouts a number, the pair whose number has been called jumps up. Players step over the legs of the others, race around the outside, then over the remaining legs and return to their original place. The first player back in place wins a point for his or her team.
4. Players must run in the direction determined by the caller and step in every space; otherwise, they are out, and the other team earns a point. The game is over when every pair has had a turn to race. The team with the most points is the winner.

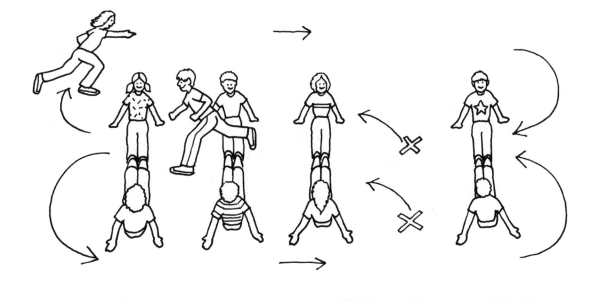

GO TAG

This tag game incorporates some clever maneuvering on the part of the chaser.

EQUIPMENT

None

SITUATION

Open space

TIME

10 minutes

DIRECTIONS

1. Everyone lines up shoulder to shoulder. Alternate players turn around and face the opposite direction, and the entire group squats down.

2. The player at one end of the line becomes the first runner. Runners may go in either direction around the line. The player at the other end is the chaser. The chaser may start in either direction but may not change direction once started.

3. Since the chaser is only allowed to run in one direction, he or she may tag a squatting player and say "Go!" The tagged player becomes the new chaser, and the chaser takes that person's place in line. In this way, all the players are part of the chase—each new chaser is able to begin from either side of the line or can start running in the opposite direction. This is a game of strategy rather than running skill.

4. When a runner is finally tagged, he or she squats at one end of the line, the chaser becomes the new runner, and the player at the other end of the line becomes the new chaser.

ROUNDABOUT

Players will have to run around in circles to win
this game.

EQUIPMENT

None

SITUATION

Open area

TIME

5 minutes

DIRECTIONS

1. Players stand in a circle facing each other front to back.
2. When the leader says "Go," everyone begins running around the
circle.
3. Always passing on the outside, each player tries to pass the person
ahead. Players try and tag players as they pass. Tagged players are out.
4. When the leader calls "Switch," players must reverse direction. This
turns the tables on the fast runner who is just about to overtake another
player.
5. The last untagged runner is the winner.

WAX MUSEUM

Here's a theatrical twist on Freeze Tag. The person who is It has the sinister mission to turn the entire group into a grisly collection of wax sculptures.

EQUIPMENT
None

SITUATION
Open area

TIME
10 minutes

DIRECTIONS
1. Select one player to be the Curator of the museum. The rest of the players are the skeptical visitors.

2. Suspicious players try to avoid the Curator. When a person is caught, he or she is instantly transformed into a hideous wax sculpture, twisted in a grotesque pose.

3. One by one, players succumb to the obsessed Curator.

4. Two players can free a wax prisoner by joining hands and encircling him or her. But players can be tagged while saving another player, and the entire trio is turned into wax!

5. The game continues until everyone is turned into wax and put on display in the museum. The last player caught becomes the Curator of the next game.

ZOMBIE

Possibly one of the most memorable and horrifying tag games is Zombie, originally invented as a street game called Chain Tag. The person who is It is a zombie in search of others to join the walking dead.

EQUIPMENT

None

SITUATION

Open area

TIME

10 minutes

DIRECTIONS

1. Select one player to be the Zombie. The Zombie wanders the earth looking for victims to join him or her.

2. When a person is caught, he or she becomes a Zombie and holds hands with the original Zombie. Together they hunt for others, and the chain becomes longer as more and more players are caught.

3. The last player to be left alive is faced with a formidable chain of pursuers chanting "Zom-bie, Zom-bie, Zom-bie." Naturally, there seems to be little hope. Will the last player become the next Zombie? We will have to wait for the sequel to see if the other Zombies are released to once again try to escape from the new wandering Zombie.

HEY - YOU'RE NOT LOOKING TOO WELL!

ZERO GRAVITY

Players will want to be lost in space to avoid being tagged. The idea of the game is simple—players cannot be tagged if they have their feet off the ground.

EQUIPMENT

None

SITUATION

Open area

TIME

10 minutes

DIRECTIONS

1. Select one player to be the earthbound mortal who cannot fly into space. Other players, with their magic zero gravity shoes, are safe as long as they can balance on a stone, hang from a tree, hug a lightpole—anything to stay off the ground.

2. The earthbound It may guard closely any player who is losing his or her grip and is soon to fall back to earth.

3. Anyone tagged while on the ground loses his or her magic shoes and becomes the new It.

LOOSE CABOOSE

With all the switching in this game, it's hard for players to stay on the right track.

EQUIPMENT

None

SITUATION

Open area

TIME

10 minutes

DIRECTIONS

1. Select a player to be the Loose Caboose. Divide the rest of the group into "trains" of three. Each player is a train car and holds the waist of the person in front. The first player in a train is the Engine.

2. The object is for the Loose Caboose to try to attach to a train. When all are aboard, the trains chug around the train yard (whistle blowing, engine chugging, and other sound effects are encouraged) trying to dodge and turn to keep away from the Caboose.

3. When the Caboose attaches to a train, the Engine of that train becomes the new Loose Caboose.

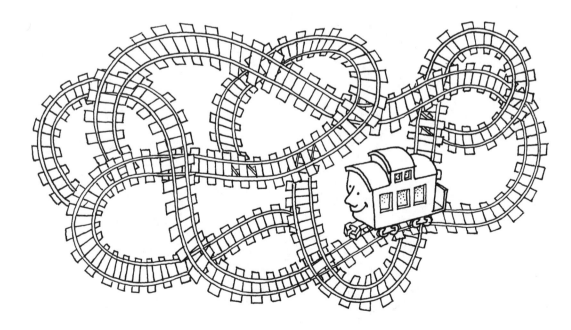

LINKS

It's a secure feeling to have ties to friends, but those connections change from time to time as demonstrated by these missing links.

EQUIPMENT

None

SITUATION

Open area

TIME

10 minutes

DIRECTIONS

1. Select one player to be It. The rest of the group forms pairs (an extra person may form a threesome).

2. Pairs link inside elbows and arrange into a single circle with It in the center. To select the missing links, It closes his or her eyes, turns around, and points to a pair of players.

3. When It says "Go," the pair breaks apart, and the two players try to link up with other pairs without being tagged. When a person links up, he or she shouts "Go," and the person on the other end of the pair must detach and run, trying to find another pair with which to link.

4. When a missing link is tagged, he or she switches places with It.

STICK UP

Players adhere to themselves as well as to the
rules in this sticky game.

EQUIPMENT

None

SITUATION

Open area

TIME

10 minutes

DIRECTIONS

1. Select one player to be Sticky Fingers. Start the game by saying "This
is a Stick Up!" as players scatter around the playground.

2. When Sticky Fingers tags a player, the tagged player must place a
hand on the place touched while still continuing to run.

3. As more and more players become "stuck" on themselves, Sticky
Fingers has a better chance to totally immobilize one player.

4. Usually when both hands of a player are stuck, the third touch sticks
him or her with being the next Sticky Fingers.

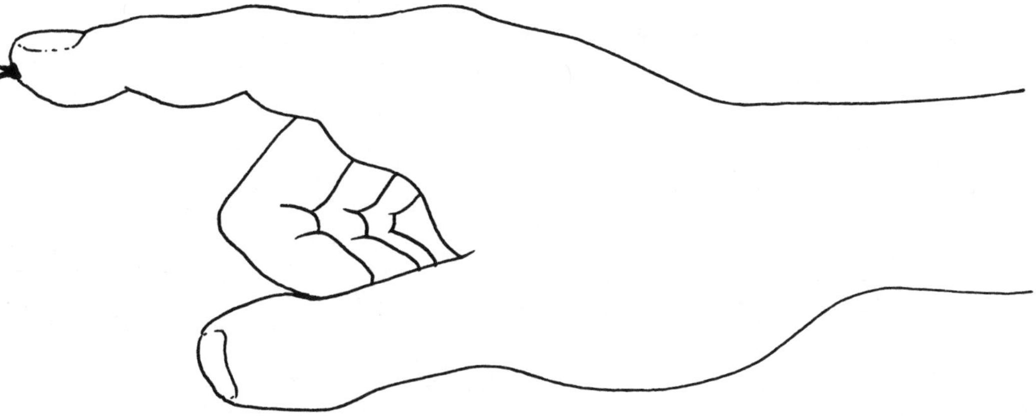

STATUE TAG

In this game, the person who is It is able to change players to stone merely by turning around.

EQUIPMENT

None

SITUATION

Open area

TIME

10 minutes

DIRECTIONS

1. Select one player to be It. Draw a start line with a stick or a piece of chalk.

2. The other players gather behind the start line while It stands 20 yards away with his or her back to the group.

3. The person who is It counts to 10 out loud as fast as possible while everyone runs or walks quickly toward him or her. As soon as 10 is reached, It turns around and players stiffen into statues and may not move. Anyone caught moving, even slightly, is sent back to the start line.

4. The person who is It turns around and counts to 10 again. The first player to get close enough tags It, and all players run back to the start line with It in pursuit.

5. Players reaching the start line are safe. If a player is tagged by It while running, he or she becomes the next It. If It fails to tag anyone, he or she continues to be It for the next round.

TAG-O-RAMA

Here's a little madness for those who appreciate tag's inherent insanity.

EQUIPMENT
None

SITUATION
Open area

TIME
5 minutes

DIRECTIONS
  1. Divide the group into pairs.
  2. Partners decide who will be It and who will be the runner.
  3. When the leader says "Go," partners begin to run around, the Its trying to tag the runners. When a partner tags the other, they switch roles. This continues until everyone feels tagged out. Despite the simplicity, players get caught up in dodging each other and trying to keep track of each other's location in the confusion. This game is particularly good as a warm-up activity for shy players.

CANCAN

In nineteenth century France, the cancan dancers of the Paris nightclubs would balance on one leg while they wiggled and kicked the other in the air. Except for this petit point, this game bears absolutely no other resemblance to the famous dance.

EQUIPMENT

2 large juice or coffee cans for each team
A piece of chalk

SITUATION

Open flat pavement

TIME

15 minutes

DIRECTIONS

1. Draw two parallel lines about 20 or 30 feet apart.
2. Divide the group into two teams, then divide each team in half. One half of each team stands behind each line on the playing field.
3. The object of the game is to move each half of each team to the opposite side of the playground. This is done using the juice cans as stepping stones.
4. To begin, the first players from each team stand on a can behind one of the lines while holding another can in one hand. When the leader says "Go," each player places the second can on the ground in front of the line and steps onto it. While balancing on this can, the players pick up the first one and put it in front to serve as the next step. If a player loses his or her balance and touches the ground, that player must start again from the beginning.
5. When players reach their team members on the other side, they place a can in back of the line for the next player to stand on to get his or her balance. The first player hops off in back of the line and hands the next player the free can. The next player cancans back across to the other side.
6. The game continues until one team has successfully switched all players from one side to the other. Then, winners are *can*gratulated!

VARIATION

Play this game as a relay race.

TIN-TYPE STILTS

Have you ever walked around with your head in the clouds? Now you can—with tin cans!

EQUIPMENT

Two large juice or coffee cans for each player
Beverage opener or hammer and nail
Ball of heavy twine
Scissors

SITUATION

Open paved area

TIME

30 minutes

DIRECTIONS

1. To construct stilts, invert two large juice or coffee cans, the closed ends on the top.

2. Punch holes on opposite sides of the top with a beverage opener or a hammer and a nail.

3. Run heavy twine through the holes and tie with a secure knot inside the can. Allow enough twine so that when players stand on can, the looped ropes reach hip height.

4. Players stand on the cans, pulling twine tightly to maintain their balance, and they are ready to stilt away.

UNOPENED BOTTOM

RUN TWINE THROUGH HOLES AND PULL KNOT INSIDE.

PUNCH HOLES USING BEVERAGE OPENER.

TIN CAN ALLEY

The biggest obstacle in this obstacle course is the tin can stilts.

EQUIPMENT

Tin can stilts for each player (see Tin-Type Stilts, page 123)
Chalk

SITUATION

Open paved area

TIME

25 minutes

DIRECTIONS

1. On a parking lot, paved playground, or long sidewalk, have the players draw an obstacle course with chalk. The course should be made for two players to use at the same time. Include lines to walk over, between, through, backward, and sideways.

2. Divide the group into two teams.

3. When the leader says "Go," one player from each team begins to walk the obstacle course while balanced on tin can stilts. Players who slip off their stilts must begin again.

4. After the first player from a team has finished, the next one may begin. The first team to complete the course is the winner.

Begin

Polka Dots

Sideways →

1 2 3 7 8 9 10 11

"can" not step!

Finish "can'd"!

Backward

TIN FOOT TWO

Two players share a tin can stilt for this three-legged race.

EQUIPMENT

3 tin can stilts for two players (see Tin-Type Stilts, page 123)

SITUATION

Open paved area

TIME

5 minutes

DIRECTIONS

1. Draw start and finish lines about 10 yards apart.

2. Divide the group into pairs.

3. Players line up at the start line with partners standing on three tin can stilts, sharing the middle stilt with their inside feet.

4. When the leader says "Go," the pairs of players race across the playground to the finish line.

5. The first pair to cross the finish line is the winner.

I THINK I CAN WALK

This community stilt extravaganza is ultimately *can*tagious.

EQUIPMENT

Enough tin can stilts to share with the entire group
  (see Tin-Type Stilts, page 123)

SITUATION

Open paved area

TIME

10 minutes

DIRECTIONS

1. Everyone lines up into a single row. Players share a tin can stilt between each other. Players on the ends will only share the stilt under their inside feet.

2. When the leader says "Go," the entire line slowly begins to move forward. The object is group cooperation and coordination.

3. Everyone wins when the group finally walks together, step by step.

VARIATION

Try a group can walk with two teams and start and finish lines. The first team to step across the finish line is the winner.

MAKING A RACKET

Tennis, badminton, and squash require special rackets. Even table tennis has it's own paddle. The games on the following pages demand one of the most unusual rackets in the world—the coat hanger racket!

EQUIPMENT

Wire coat hanger for each player
Old nylon stocking or pantyhose for each player
Several rolls of masking tape

SITUATION

Small flat area

TIME

20 minutes

DIRECTIONS

1. Give each player a wire coat hanger and an old nylon stocking. Supply the group with several rolls of masking tape to share.

2. Have players pull hangers into a diamond shape and straighten the hook.

3. Push the hanger into the nylon stocking, making sure it fits snugly into the toe. Pull the stocking tightly over the hanger to form a taut net. Gather the loose end by twisting it around the handle and taping it to the handle.

4. Bend half the hook of the hanger back to the base of the diamond. Twist tape around the entire wire to form a handle, and you are ready to play.

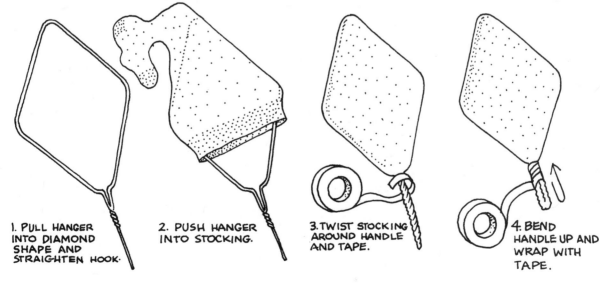

1. PULL HANGER INTO DIAMOND SHAPE AND STRAIGHTEN HOOK.

2. PUSH HANGER INTO STOCKING.

3. TWIST STOCKING AROUND HANDLE AND TAPE.

4. BEND HANDLE UP AND WRAP WITH TAPE.

RACKET SQUAD

Balancing a balloon is a breeze—but only when it isn't breezy.

EQUIPMENT

Coat hanger racket for each player (see Making a Racket, page 127)
Balloon for each player

SITUATION

Open area

TIME

10 minutes

DIRECTIONS

1. Mark start and finish lines about 10 yards apart. Each player takes a balloon, blows it up, and ties a knot in it.
2. Players line up at the start line with balloons balanced on their wire rackets.
3. When the leader says "Go," players begin to walk quickly toward the finish line, balancing their balloons without letting them blow off. Players may not use hands to touch balloons; however, if a balloon falls off, the player stops, picks up the balloon, counts to three, and continues.
4. The first player to cross the finish line with the balloon on the racket is the winner.

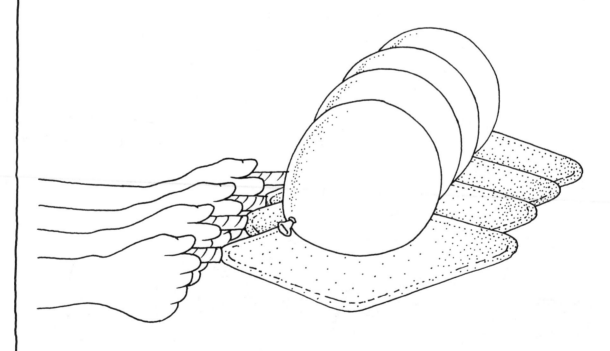

BALLOON TENNIS RACE

Pairs of players try to maintain their stride and their volley as they move across the playing field.

EQUIPMENT

Coat hanger racket for each player (see Making a Racket, page 127)
Balloon for each pair of players

SITUATION

Open area

TIME

10 minutes

DIRECTIONS

1. Mark start and finish lines about 10 yards apart.
2. Divide the group into pairs. Each should have two rackets and a balloon.
3. When the leader says "Go," partners begin walking, hitting the balloon back and forth while trying to maneuver to the finish line. Players have to direct their balloons while avoiding other balloon batters.
4. The first pair of players to cross the finish line is the winner.

POP STOP

This is a game of combative strategy, placing players on the offensive and defensive at the same time.

EQUIPMENT

A balloon for each player
Ball of string
Scissors

SITUATION

Large open area

TIME

10 minutes

DIRECTIONS

  1. Give each player a balloon to blow up and a piece of string with which to tie the balloon to his or her right ankle.
  2. At the signal of the leader, a player must try to burst as many of the other players' balloons as possible without having his or her own balloon popped. It will take careful maneuvering and skill to try to protect a balloon while attacking other balloons.
  3. Those whose balloons have popped should step aside to watch the survivors stomp and pop.
  4. The last player with an unpopped balloon is the winner and gets to pop it.

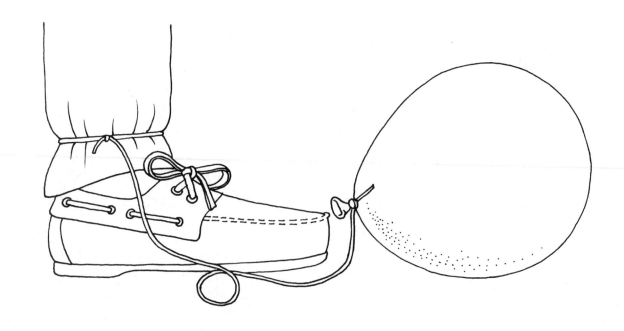

VOLLEY FOLLY

Pairs work together to keep the longest volley
going.

EQUIPMENT

Coat hanger racket for each player (see Making a
Racket, page 127)
Newspaper
Roll of masking tape
Piece of chalk or length of rope

SITUATION

Open area

TIME

15 minutes

DIRECTIONS

1. This game is played with newspaper balls. Players make them by
crushing a piece of newspaper and wrapping it with masking tape.

2. Make an instant playing court by drawing a chalk line down the middle
of the pavement or by stretching a rope across the grass.

3. Divide the group into partners, each partner facing the other on either
side of the line. Try to keep enough space between players so that
partners do not interfere with the players to either side. If the group is very
large, divide it into smaller groups to take turns.

4. The object of the game is to see which pair can volley the longest
without missing the newspaper ball. When the leader says "Go," partners
begin to hit newspaper balls back and forth. When a volley begins, players
keep count.

5. The pair with the largest number of volleys is the winner. In case of a
tie, have partners take a step backward and begin again until one pair
volleys the longest.

THE GAME GAME

Here's a game where creating the game is the game. Now if you didn't quite follow that, look at it this way—you need to play the game in order to play the game. Now isn't that clearer?

EQUIPMENT

6 medium-sized cardboard boxes
Tempera paint—black and white or any two contrasting colors
Masking tape
Brushes
Cups for paint

SITUATION

Open area

TIME

60 minutes

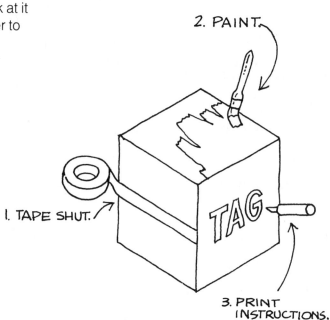

2. PAINT.

1. TAPE SHUT.

3. PRINT INSTRUCTIONS.

DIRECTIONS

1. The object of this activity is to design a game and then to play it. Every game is a combination of various elements which when put together in different ways create an entirely new game. Some elements emphasize fantasy, others skill, while others are built around a piece of equipment. In this game, players first play with the elements that make up the game.

2. Game elements are:

- Objectives or goals to reach: to create a group dance, to tag another player, to win a race, to throw the farthest, to guess an answer, to pretend you are someone else, to move imperceptively
- Types of activity: sitting, running, jumping, crawling, dancing, pantomime
- Structure and organization: circles, safety zones, start and finish lines, lines of players, scattered players, tight huddle
- Props: balls or balloons, ropes, boxes, Frisbees, paper or fabric, none
- Roles: two teams, three teams, partners, the whole group, It, individual players
- Attitude or theme: TV characters, outer space, monsters, being invisible, numbers, chants, ritual handshakes, songs

3. To prepare, collect six boxes and tape them closed. Paint each box a solid color.

4. Each box represents an element. Paint six various options for each element on each side of the boxes. For example, one box might read "tag, race, throw, guess, pretend, and stand still"—one option on each side.

5. Divide the group into two teams. Each team is given a turn to throw all six boxes. The words that appear on top of each box must be incorporated into a game. For example, the game might have to be a race, with three teams, in a circle, while singing, and using a balloon.

6. Each team has five minutes to create a game, which is then shared with the entire group. There are no official winner or losers, but everyone will know which one they enjoyed the most.

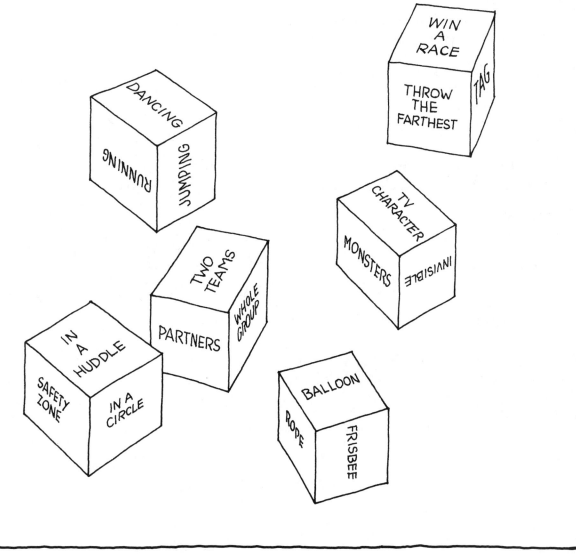

THE GREAT BICYCLE EXPO

Most kids have their own bikes, and this tournament promotes safe skills rather than dangerous stunts. Set up a course in a place away from cars—for example, in a parking lot when it is not in use. After the races, celebrate with a colorful parade of fabulous bike floats.

The Coasting Contest

EQUIPMENT

A piece of chalk

TIME

10 minutes

PEDAL 10 YARDS. THE LONGEST COAST WINS.

DIRECTIONS

1. With a piece of chalk, draw start and coasting lines about 10 yards apart. Racers, seated on their bikes, line up at the start line.
2. On a signal from the leader, the racers pedal as hard as possible toward the coasting line.
3. At the coasting line, players stop pedaling and coast. The racer who coasts the furthest wins.

IT'S TAKEN HIM 49 YEARS TO PEDAL FROM THE CORNER!

Snail Trail Test

EQUIPMENT

A piece of chalk

TIME

10 minutes

DIRECTIONS

1. Draw start and finish lines about 10 yards apart with a piece of chalk. Racers line up at the start line mounted on their bikes.
2. On a signal from the leader, the racers go as slowly as possible to the finish line. Players must balance on their bikes, and anyone who puts a foot on the ground is out.
3. The last rider to get to the finish line is the winner.

Obstacle Course Competition

EQUIPMENT

A piece of chalk
8 or 9 large tin cans or empty milk containers

TIME

15 minutes

DIRECTIONS

1. Draw a path about 5 inches wide and 50 feet long.

2. Collect eight or nine large juice cans or empty milk cartons. Weight them down by filling them with stones. Alternately place the cans or cartons a few inches on either side of the line and about six feet from each other.

3. One by one, riders ride down the middle of the path. Points are given for going off the path and for touching obstacles.

4. The rider with the least number of points and the fastest time is the winner.

The Slalom Race

EQUIPMENT

A piece of chalk
8 or 9 large tin cans or empty milk containers

TIME

15 minutes

DIRECTIONS

1. Arrange the cans or cartons on the obstacle course into a straight line. Space between the obstacles can be varied to make the course easier, more difficult, or more interesting.

2. One by one, riders weave in and out around the obstacles. Points are given for touching obstacles and for putting a foot on the ground.

3. The rider with the least number of points and fastest time is the winner.

VARIATION

Remove the stones from the containers. Players must touch the containers without knocking them over.

The Toss-In Race

EQUIPMENT

4 or 5 empty boxes or wastepaper cans
4 or 5 small balls, marbles, or bean bags

TIME

15 minutes

DIRECTIONS

1. Arrange four or five empty boxes or wastepaper cans about eight feet apart in a zigzag course.

2. Riders begin by holding four or five balls, marbles, or beanbags (depending on the number of containers) in one hand. When the leader gives the signal, riders weave in and out around the boxes or cans, dropping a marble or ball in each.

3. The rider who gets the most objects into the containers in the shortest time is the winner.

VARIATION

Try a Pick-Up Race by inverting containers and placing objects on top. The winner is the player who can pick up the most objects without dropping them in the shortest amount of time.

Quick Stop Finish

EQUIPMENT

A piece of chalk

TIME

10 minutes

DIRECTIONS

1. Draw start and finish lines about 25 feet apart.

2. Riders line up on the start line. When the signal is given, everyone zooms toward the finish line.

3. The winner is the first rider to get to the finish line by stopping the closest without skidding. Riders can shift their weight to the rear after brakes have been applied to help prevent skidding.

Balancing the Books

EQUIPMENT

An old book for each rider

TIME

10 minutes

DIRECTIONS

1. You'll need to find an old, unimportant book for each player. Each player balances a book on his or her head.

2. On a signal from the leader, players ride around in any direction, trying to keep the books perched on their heads.

3. The player who rides the longest while keeping the book on his or her head is the winner.

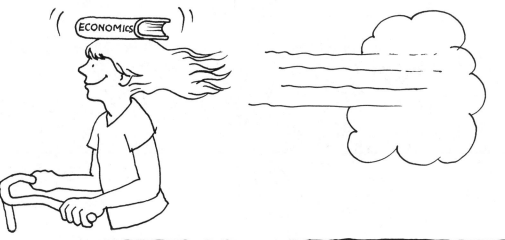

BIKE BEAUTIES

Now that the competition is over, players are ready to show off their winning wheels.

EQUIPMENT

Rolls of crepe paper in various colors
Colored construction paper
Scissors
A playing card for each player
A clip-style clothespin for each player
Several rolls of reflective tape in various colors

SITUATION

Open paved area

TIME

25 minutes

DIRECTIONS

Wheel Weavings

Cut strips of different colors of crepe paper into shorter lengths so that players can slip them between the spokes. Players weave the crepe paper in and out to create a rainbow of color, and they're ready to roll. For added variation, shapes can be cut from construction paper—long squiggles, stars, zigzags, and so forth—and slipped between the spokes.

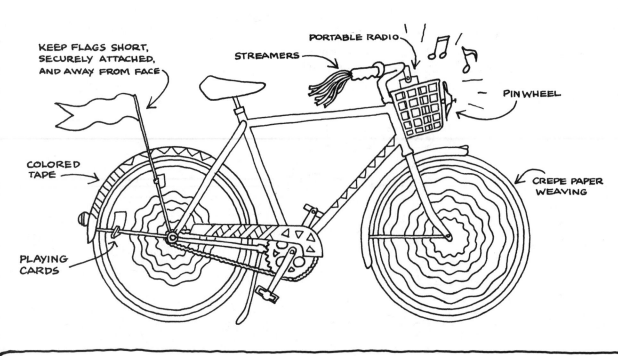

KEEP FLAGS SHORT, SECURELY ATTACHED, AND AWAY FROM FACE

PORTABLE RADIO

STREAMERS

PINWHEEL

COLORED TAPE

CREPE PAPER WEAVING

PLAYING CARDS

Riding Racket

This is an old trick that changes a quiet bikester into a noisy nuisance. All each player needs is a playing card and a clip-style clothespin. Clip the card to the rear fender brace with the tip of the card between the spokes. Then pedal away, clattering into the sunset.

Fancy Fenders

Add your own decorative touch to fenders with some reflective tape, which can be purchased at bicycle shops or automotive stores. Cut tape into strips and stick them on. Arrange strips into a V-shaped chevron or a criss-cross of different colors. These designs not only make bikes look nice in the daylight but also act as safety reflectors at night.

Finishing Touches

To complete the Bike Beauties, players can add streams of crepe paper to the hand grips and the rear fender. Pinwheels can be mounted on the handlebars (see Wheels on Wheels, page 37), and construction paper flags can be taped to sticks and attached as in motorcycle escorts. Organize all the bikes in a drill team of bike formations—and don't forget the portable radios! Set several radios to the same station to create a bike band.

ABOUT THE AUTHOR

As an artist and designer, Bob Gregson has created playful programs for more than 10 years. He's directed the art classes for the Wadsworth Atheneum in Hartford, Connecticut; taught at the Young Artists Studios in Chicago; and designed participatory programs and exhibits for the Art Institute of Chicago and the Capital Children's Museum in Washington, D.C. As cofounder of Sidewalk, Inc. in Hartford, Bob helped organize a yearly Play Day, a large-scale community festival which is a model of collective creativity. He developed the Activity Truck, a mobile playground which transforms neighborhoods into festivals in an instant. Bob has produced inventive media events for television and radio and is currently working as the Cultural Planner for the City of New Haven, planning programs to make the city more fun. He is also the author and illustrator of the *Incredible Indoor Games Book*.